Beyond Vision and LANguage: inTEgrating Real-world kNowledge (LANTERN 2019)

Hong Kong, China
3 November 2019

ISBN: 978-1-7138-0082-8

EMNLP-IJCNLP 2019

**Beyond Vision and LANguage: inTEgrating Real-world kNowledge
(LANTERN)**

Proceedings of the Workshop

November 3, 2019
Hong Kong, China

Introduction

Welcome to The First Workshop Beyond Vision and Language: Integrating Real-World Knowledge (LANTERN) co-located with EMNLP-IJCNLP 2019. The primary goal of the workshop is to bring together researchers adopting machine learning techniques to interconnect language, vision, and other modalities by leveraging external knowledge. By encouraging contributions exploiting very diverse sources of external knowledge (knowledge graphs, fixed and dynamic environments, cognitive and neuroscience data, etc.), the workshop aims to foster discussion and promote novel research directions which acknowledge the importance of knowledge in acquiring, using, and evaluating language in real-world settings.

In this first edition, we called for both long and short papers. All the accepted ones are published in these Proceedings.

LANTERN 2019 received 17 submissions, out of which 1 was desk-rejected before the reviewing phase due to inappropriateness. The remaining 16 papers received 2 highly-qualified double-blind reviews. Besides considering the average overall score, only papers for which none of the reviewers expressed a negative opinion (strong or weak reject) were accepted. In total, 9 papers (3 long, 6 short) were accepted to appear in the workshop, with an acceptance rate of around 53%.

Contributions are representative of a varied number of current problems and approaches and include novel deep learning techniques and tasks in the domain of visual reasoning, the use of multilingual embeddings and scene graphs in multimodal tasks, multi-agent language learning, the use of eye tracking data in syntactic tagging and of textual adversaries in multimodal machine translation, the extraction of orthography knowledge from Chinese characters. Such richness of approaches and perspectives is in line with the purpose of the workshop, and confirms the growing interest for problems going beyond the task-specific integration of language and vision.

The program of the workshop, besides 4 oral presentations and a poster session, includes 3 invited talks by Lucia Specia, Mohit Bansal, and Siddharth Narayanaswamy. The workshop received sponsorship by iDeaL SFB 1102 and Nuance. Best paper and best poster awards are sponsored by SAP.

The LANTERN Workshop Organizers

Organizers:

Aditya Mogadala, Saarland University (Germany)
Dietrich Klakow, Saarland University (Germany)
Sandro Pezzelle, University of Amsterdam (The Netherlands)
Marie-Francine Moens, Katholieke Universiteit Leuven (Belgium)

Program Committee:

Spandana Gella, Amazon AI
Ravi Shekhar, Queen Mary University London
Angeliki Lazaridou, DeepMind
Ionut-Teodor Sorodoc, Universitat Pompeu Fabra
Niket Tandon, Allen Institute for Artificial Intelligence (AI2)
Florian Metze, CMU
Alexander Kuhnle, Cambridge University
Mirella Lapata, Edinburgh University
Mario Fritz, CISPA, Saarland
Carina Silberer, Universitat Pompeu Fabra
Barbara Plank, IT University of Copenhagen
Jacob Goldberger, Bar Ilan
Pranava Madhyastha, Imperial College London
Stefan Lee, Oregon State University
Parisa Kordjamshidi, Michigan State University

Invited Speaker:

Mohit Bansal, UNC Chapel Hill
Lucia Specia, Imperial College London
Siddharth Narayanaswamy, Oxford Univeristy

Table of Contents

Conference Program

LANTERN is a half-day event with four oral and five spotlight presentations for the accepted long and short papers. It also includes three invited presentations. The full schedule is presented below.

14:00–14:15 Welcome and Opening Remarks

14:15–14:45 Invited Talk: Lucia Specia (Imperial College London)

Session 1: Accepted Papers (Oral)

14:45–15:00 On the Role of Scene Graphs in Image Captioning

15:00–15:15 Learning to request guidance in emergent language

15:15–15:30 Spotlight (posters)

- Aligning Multilingual Word Embeddings for Cross-Modal Retrieval Task
- Big Generalizations with Small Data: Exploring the Role of Training Samples in Learning Adjectives of Size
- Eigencharacter: An Embedding of Chinese Character Orthography
- Understanding the Effect of Textual Adversaries in Multimodal Machine Translation
- Seeded self-play for language learning

15:30–16:15 Coffee Break with Poster Session

16:15–16:45 Invited Talk: Siddharth Narayanaswamy (Oxford University)

Session 2: Accepted Papers (Oral)

16:45–17:00 At a Glance: The Impact of Gaze Aggregation Views on Syntactic Tagging

17:00–17:15 Structure Learning for Neural Module Networks

17:15–17:45 Invited Talk: Mohit Bansal (UNC Chapel Hill)

17:45–18:00 Best Talk/Poster Award and Concluding Remarks

Structure Learning for Neural Module Networks

Vardaan Pahuja[◦*]　　**Jie Fu**[†‡]　　**Sarath Chandar**[†§]　　**Christopher J. Pal**[†‡]

[†]Mila　　[§]Université de Montréal
[‡]Polytechnique Montréal　　[◦]The Ohio State University

Abstract

Neural Module Networks, originally proposed
for the task of visual question answering, are
a class of neural network architectures that involve human-specified neural modules, each
designed for a specific form of reasoning. In
current formulations of such networks only the
parameters of the neural modules and/or the order of their execution is learned. In this work,
we further expand this approach and also learn
the underlying internal structure of modules in
terms of the ordering and combination of simple and elementary arithmetic operators. We
utilize a minimum amount of prior knowledge
from the human-specified neural modules in
the form of different input types and arithmetic
operators used in these modules. Our results
show that one is indeed able to simultaneously
learn both internal module structure and module sequencing without extra supervisory signals for module execution sequencing. With
this approach, we report performance comparable to models using hand-designed modules.
In addition, we do a analysis of sensitivity of
the learned modules w.r.t. the arithmetic operations and infer the analytical expressions of
the learned modules.

1 Introduction

Designing general purpose reasoning modules is
one of the central challenges in artificial intelligence. Neural Module Networks (Andreas et al.,
2016b) were introduced as a general purpose visual reasoning architecture and have been shown to
work well for the task of visual question answering
(Antol et al., 2015; Malinowski and Fritz, 2014;
Ren et al., 2015b,a). They use dynamically com-
posable modules which are then assembled into
a layout based on syntactic parse of the question.

The modules take as input the images or the attention maps[1] and return attention maps or labels
as output. In (Hu et al., 2017), the layout prediction is relaxed by learning a layout policy with a
sequence-to-sequence RNN. This layout policy is
jointly trained along with the parameters of the
modules. The model proposed in (Hu et al., 2018)
avoids the use of reinforcement learning to train the
layout predictor, and uses soft program execution
to learn both layout and module parameters jointly.

A fundamental limitation of these previous modular approaches to visual reasoning is that the modules need to be hand-specified. This might not
be feasible when one has limited knowledge of
the kinds of questions or associated visual reasoning required to solve the task. In this work, we
present an approach to learn the module structure,
along with the parameters of the modules in an
end-to-end differentiable training setting. Our proposed model, Learnable Neural Module Network
(LNMN), learns the structure of the module, the
parameters of the module, and the way to compose
the modules based on just the regular task loss.
Our results show that we can learn the structure of
the modules automatically and still perform com-
parably to hand-specified modules. We want to
highlight the fact that our goal in this paper is not
to beat the performance of the hand-specified modules since they are specifically engineered for the
task. Instead, our goal is to explore the possibility
of designing general-purpose reasoning modules in
an entirely data-driven fashion.

2 Background

In this section, we describe the working of the
Stack-NMN model (Hu et al., 2018) as our proposed
LNMN model uses this as the base model. The

---

[*]Corresponding author: Vardaan Pahuja <vardaan-
pahuja@gmail.com> Work done when the author was a student at Mila, Université de Montréal.

[1]An attention map denotes a $H \times W \times 1$ tensor which
assigns a saliency score to the convolutional features in the
spatial dimension.

Proceedings of the Beyond Vision and LANguage: inTEgrating Real-world kNowledge (LANTERN), pages 1–10
Hong Kong, China, November 3, 2019. ©2019 Association for Computational Linguistics

Stack-NMN model is an end-to-end differentiable model for the task of Visual Question Answering and Referential Expression Grounding (Rohrbach et al., 2016). It addresses a major drawback of prior visual reasoning models in the literature that compositional reasoning is implemented without the need of supervisory signals for composing the layout at training time. It consists of several hand-specified modules (namely Find, Transform, And, Or, Filter, Scene, Answer, Compare and NoOp) which are parameterized, differentiable, and implement common routines needed in visual reasoning and learns to compose them without strong supervision. The implementation details of these modules are given in Appendix A.2 (see Table 8). The different sub-components of the Stack-NMN model are described below.

2.1 Module Layout Controller

The structure of the controller is similar to the one proposed in (Hudson and Manning, 2018). The controller first encodes the question using a bi-directional LSTM (Hochreiter and Schmidhuber, 1997). Let $[h_1, h_2, ..., h_S]$ denote the output of Bi-LSTM at each time-step of the input sequence of question words. Let q denote the concatenation of final hidden state of Bi-LSTM during the forward and backward passes. q can be considered as the encoding of the entire question. The controller executes the modules iteratively for T times. At each time-step, the updated query representation u is obtained as:

$$u = W_2[W_1^{(t)}q + b_1; c_{t-1}] + b_2$$

where $W_1^{(t)} \in \mathbb{R}^{d \times d}$, $W_2 \in \mathbb{R}^{d \times 2d}$, $b_1 \in \mathbb{R}^d$, $b_2 \in \mathbb{R}^d$ are controller parameters. c_{t-1} is the textual parameter from the previous time step. The controller has two outputs viz. the textual parameter at step t (denoted by c_t) and the attention on each module (denoted by vector $w^{(t)}$). The controller first predicts an attention $cv_{t,s}$ on each of the words of the question and then uses this attention to do a weighted average over the outputs of the Bi-LSTM.

$$cv_{t,s} = softmax(W_3(u \odot h_s))$$

$$c_t = \sum_{s=1}^{S} cv_{t,s} \cdot h_s$$

where, $W_3 \in \mathbb{R}^{1 \times d}$ is another controller parameter. The attention on each module $w^{(t)}$ is obtained by

feeding the query representation at each time-step to a Multi-layer Perceptron (MLP).

$$w^{(t)} = softmax(MLP(u; \theta_{MLP}))$$

2.2 Operation of Memory Stack for storing attention maps

In order to answer a visual reasoning question, the model needs to execute modules in a tree-structured layout. In order to facilitate this sort of compositional behavior, a differentiable memory pool to store and retrieve intermediate attention maps is used. A memory stack (with length denoted by L) stores $H \times W$ dimensional attention maps, where H and W are the height and width of image feature maps respectively. Depending on the number of attention maps required as input by the module, it pops them from the stack and later pushes the result back to the stack. The model performs soft module execution by executing all modules at each time step. The updated stack and stack

---

Data: Question (string), Image features ($\mathcal{I}$)
Encode the input question into
  d-dimensional sequence $[h_1, h_2, ..., h_S]$
  using Bidirectional LSTM.
$A^{(0)} \leftarrow$ Initialize the memory stack $(A; p)$
  with uniform image attention and set the
  stack pointer p to point at the bottom of the
  stack (one-hot vector with 1 in the 1st
  dim.).
for *each time-step t = 0, 1, ..., (T-1)* **do**
  $u = W_2[W_1^{(t)}q + b_1; c_{t-1}] + b_2$;
  $w^{(t)} = softmax(MLP(u; \theta_{MLP}))$;
  $cv_{t,s} = softmax(W_3(u \odot h_s))$;
  $c_t = \sum_{s=1}^{S} cv_{t,s} \cdot h_s$
  for *every module $m \in M$* **do**
    Produce updated stack and stack
    pointer: $(A_m^{(t)}, p_m^{(t)}) =$
    run-module$(m, A^{(t)}, p^{(t)}, c_t, \mathcal{I})$;
  end
  $A^{(t+1)} = \sum_{m \in M} A_m^{(t)} \cdot w_m^{(t)}$;
  $p^{(t+1)} = softmax(\sum_{m \in M} p_m^{(t)} \cdot w_m^{(t)})$
end

Algorithm 1: Operation of Module Layout Controller and Memory Stack.

---

pointer at each subsequent time-step are obtained by a weighted average of those corresponding to each module using the weights $w^{(t)}$ predicted by the module controller. This is illustrated by the equations below:

$$(A_m^{(t)}, p_m^{(t)}) = \text{run-module}(m, A^{(t)}, p^{(t)})$$

$$A^{(t+1)} = \sum_{m \in M} A_m^{(t)} \cdot w_m^{(t)}$$

$$p^{(t+1)} = softmax(\sum_{m \in M} p_m^{(t)} \cdot w_m^{(t)})$$

Here, $A_m^{(t)}$ and $p_m^{(t)}$ denote the stack and stack pointer respectively, after executing module m at time-step t. $A^{(t)}$ and $p^{(t)}$ denote the stack and stack pointer obtained after the weighted average of those corresponding to all modules at previous time-step $(t-1)$. The working of module layout controller and its interfacing with memory stack is illustrated in Algorithm 1. The implementation details of operation of the stack are shown in Appendix (see Algorithm 3).

2.3 Final Classifier

At each time step of module execution, the weighted average of output of the *Answer* modules is called memory features (denoted by $f_{mem}^{(t)} = \sum_{m \in \text{ans. module}} o_m^{(t)} w_m^{(t)}$). Here, $o_m^{(t)}$ denotes the output of module m at time t. The memory features are given as one of the inputs to the *Answer* modules at the next time-step. The memory features at the final time-step are concatenated with the question representation, and then fed to an MLP to obtain the logits.

3 Learnable Neural Module Networks

In this section, we introduce Learnable Neural Module Networks (LNMNs) for visual reasoning, which extends Stack-NMN. However, the modules in LNMN are not hand-specified. Rather, they are generic modules as specified below.

3.1 Structure of the Generic Module

The *cell* (see Figures 1 and 2) denotes a generic module, which we suppose can span all the required modules for a visual reasoning task. Each cell contains a certain number of nodes. The function of a node (denoted by O) is to perform a weighted sum of outputs of different arithmetic operations applied on the input feature maps x_1 and x_2. Let $\alpha' = \sigma(\alpha)$ denote the output of softmax

function applied to the vector α such that

$$O(x_1, x_2) = \alpha_1' * min(x_1, x_2)$$
$$+ \alpha_2' * max(x_1, x_2) + \alpha_3' * (x_1 + x_2) +$$
$$\alpha_4' * (x_1 \odot x_2) + \alpha_5' * choose_1(x_1, x_2)$$
$$+ \alpha_6' * choose_2(x_1, x_2)$$

All of the above operations (*min*, *max*, +, $\odot$) are element-wise operations. The last two non-standard functions are defined as: $choose_1(x_1, x_2) = x_1$ and $choose_2(x_1, x_2) = x_2$.

We consider two broad kinds of modules: (i) *Attention modules* which output an attention map (ii) *Answer modules* which output memory features to be stored in the memory. Among each of these two categories, there is a finer categorization:

3.1.1 Generic Module with 3 inputs

This module type receives 3 inputs (i.e. image features, textual parameter, and a single attention map) and produces a single output. The first node receives input from the image feature ($\mathcal{I}$) and the attention map (popped from the memory stack). The second node receives input from the textual parameter followed by a linear layer ($W_1 c_{txt}$), and the output of the first node.

3.1.2 Generic Module with 4 inputs

This module type receives 4 inputs (i.e. image features, textual parameter and two attention maps) and produces a single output. The first node receives the two attention maps, each of which are popped from the memory stack, as input. The second node receives input from the image features along with the output of the first node. The third node receives input from the textual parameter followed by a linear layer, and the output of the second node.

For the *Attention* modules, the output of the final node is converted into a single-channel attention map using a 1×1 convolutional layer. For the *Answer* modules, the output of the final node is summed over spatial dimensions, and the resulting feature vector is concatenated with memory features of previous time-step and textual parameter features, fed to a linear layer to output memory features. The schematic diagrams of *Answer* modules are given in the Appendix A.1 (see Figures 6, 7).

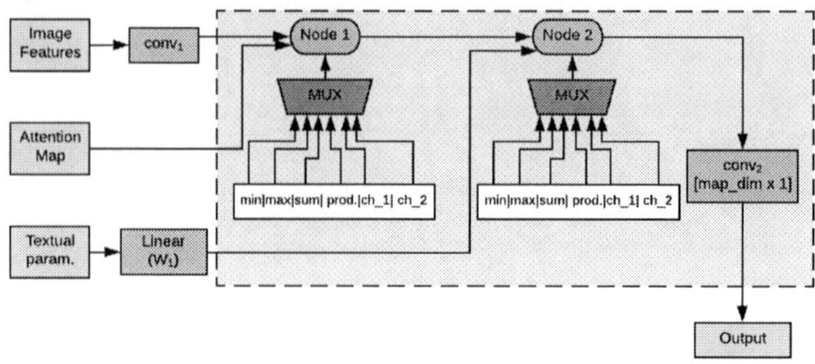

Figure 1: Attention Module schematic diagram (3 inputs).

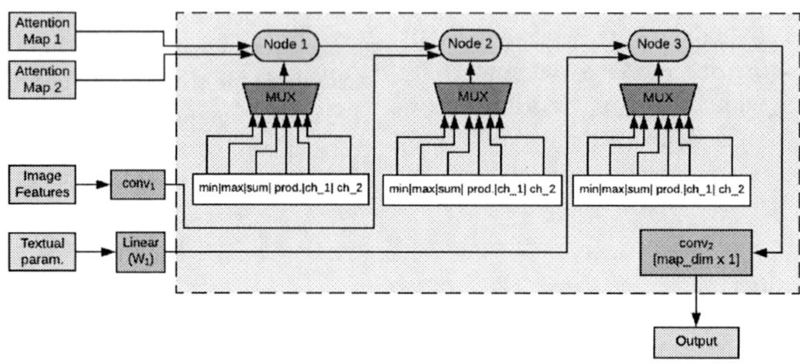

Figure 2: Attention Module schematic diagram (4 inputs).

3.2 Overall structure

The structure of our end-to-end model extends *Stack-NMN* in that we specify each module in terms of the generic module (defined in Section 3.1). We experiment with three model ablations in terms of number of modules for each type being used. See Table 3 for details[2]. We train the module structure parameters (denoted by $\alpha = \left\{\alpha_i^{m,k}\right\}_{i=1}^{6}$ for k^{th} node of module m) and the weight parameters ($\mathcal{W}$) by adopting alternating gradient descent steps in architecture and weight spaces respectively. For a particular epoch, the gradient step in weight space is performed on each training batch, and the gradient step in architecture space is performed on a batch randomly sampled from the validation set. This is done to ensure that we find an architecture corresponding to the modules which has a low validation loss on the updated weight parameters. This is inspired by the technique used in (Liu et al., 2018) to learn monolithic architectures like CNNs and RNNs in terms of basic building blocks (or *cells*). Algorithm 2 illustrates the training algorithm. Here, $\mathcal{L}_{train}(\mathcal{W}, \alpha)$ and $\mathcal{L}_{val}(\mathcal{W}, \alpha)$ denote the training

while *not converged* **do**

    1. Update weights $\mathcal{W}$ by descending

$$\nabla_w \left[\mathcal{L}_{train}(\mathcal{W}, \alpha) - \frac{\lambda_w}{T} \sum_{t=1}^{T} \mathcal{H}(w^{(t)}) \right]$$

    2. Update architecture α by descending

$$\nabla_\alpha \left[\mathcal{L}_{val}(\mathcal{W}, \alpha) - \right.$$
$$\left. \lambda_{op} \sum_{m=1}^{M} \sum_{k=1}^{p} \frac{\left\| \sigma(\alpha^{m,k}) \right\|_2}{\left\| \sigma(\alpha^{m,k}) \right\|_1} \right]$$

end

Algorithm 2: Training Algorithm for LNMN Modules. Here, α denotes the collection of module network parameters i.e. $\left\{\alpha_i^{m,k}\right\}_{i=1}^{6}$ for k^{th} node of module m, $\mathcal{W}$ denotes the collection of weight parameters of modules and all other non-module parameters.

---

[2] 1 NoOp module is included by default in all ablations.

loss and validation loss on the combination of parameters $(\mathcal{W}, \boldsymbol{\alpha})$ respectively. For the gradient step on the training batch, we add an additional loss term to initially maximize the entropy of $w^{(t)}$ and gradually anneal the regularization coefficient (λ_w) to the opposite sign (which minimizes the entropy of $w^{(t)}$ towards the end of training). The value of λ_w varies linearly from 1.0 to 0.0 in the first 20 epochs and then steeply decreases to -1.0 in next 10 epochs. The trend of variation of λ_w is shown in Appendix (see Figure 5). For the gradient steps in the architecture space, we add an additional loss term ($\frac{l2}{l1} = \frac{\|\sigma(\alpha)\|_2}{\|\sigma(\alpha)\|_1}$) (Hurley and Rickard, 2009) to encourage the sparsity of module structure parameters ($\boldsymbol{\alpha}$) after the softmax activation.

4   Experiments

We train our model on the CLEVR visual reasoning task. CLEVR (Johnson et al., 2017a) is a synthetic dataset for visual reasoning containing around 700K examples, and has become the standard benchmark to test visual reasoning models. It contains questions that test visual reasoning abilities such as counting, comparing, logical reasoning based on 3D shapes like cubes, spheres, and cylinders of varied shades. A typical example question and image pair from this dataset is given in Appendix (see Figure 4). The results on CLEVR test set are reported in Table 1. Some ablations of the model are shown in Table 2. We use the pre-trained CLEVR model to fine-tune the model on CLEVR-Humans dataset. The latter is a dataset of challenging human-posed questions based on a much larger vocabulary on the same CLEVR images. The corresponding results are shown in Table 1 (see last column). In addition, we experiment on VQA v1 (Antol et al., 2015) and VQA v2 (Goyal et al., 2017) which are VQA datasets containing natural images. The results for VQA v1 and VQA v2 are shown in Table 4.

The detailed accuracy for each question sub-type for the VQA datasets is given in Appendix A.4 (see Tables 9 and 10). We use Adam (Kingma and Ba, 2014) as the optimizer for the weight parameters with a learning rate of 1e$-$4, $(\beta_1, \beta_2) = (0.9, 0.999)$ and no weight decay. For the module network parameters, we use the same optimizer with a different learning rate 3e$-$4, $(\beta_1, \beta_2) = (0.5, 0.999)$ and a weight decay of 1e$-$3. The value of λ_{op} is set to 1.0. The code for implementation

of our model is available online[3].

4.1   Results

The comparison of CLEVR overall accuracy shows that our model (LNMN (9 modules)) receives only a slight dip (1.53%) compared to the Stack-NMN model. We also experiment with other variants of our model in which we increase the number of *Answer* modules (LNMN (11 modules)) and/or *Attention* modules (LNMN (14 modules)). The LNMN (11 modules) model performs better than the other two ablations (0.89% accuracy drop w.r.t. the Stack-NMN model). For the 'Count' and 'Compare Numbers' sub-category of questions, all of the 3 variants perform consistently better than the Stack-NMN model. In case of CLEVR-Humans dataset, the accuracy drop is a modest 1.71%. Even for the natural image VQA datasets, our approach has comparable results with the Stack-NMN model. The results clearly show that the modules learned by our model (in terms of elementary arithmetic operations) perform approximately as well as the ones specified in the Stack-NMN model (that contains hand-designed modules which were tailor-made for the CLEVR dataset). The results from the ablations in Table 2 show that a naive concatenation of all inputs to a module (or *cell*) results in a poor performance (around 47 %). Thus, the structure we propose to fuse the inputs plays a key role in model performance. When we replace the $\boldsymbol{\alpha}$ vector for each node by a one-hot vector during inference, the drop in accuracy is only 1.79% which shows that the learned distribution over operation weights peaks over a specific operation which is desirable.

4.2   Measuring the sensitivity of modules

We use an attribution technique called Integrated Gradients (Sundararajan et al., 2017) to study the impact of module structure parameters (denoted by $\left\{\alpha_i^{m,k}\right\}_{i=1}^{6}$ for k^{th} node of module m) on the probability distribution in the last layer of LNMN model. Let $\mathcal{I}_j$ and q_j denote the (image, question) pairs for the jth example. Let $F(\mathcal{I}_j, q_j, \boldsymbol{\alpha})$ denote the function that assigns the probability corresponding to the correct answer index in the softmax distribution. Here, $\alpha_i^{m,k}$ denotes the module network parameter for the ith operator in k^{th} node of module m. Then, the attribution of $[\alpha_1^m, \alpha_2^m, \alpha_3^m, \alpha_4^m, \alpha_5^m, \alpha_6^m]$ (summed across all nodes $k = 1, ..., p$ for a particular module m and

---

[3]`https://github.com/vardaan123/LNMN`

Model	CLEVR Overall	Count	Exist	Compare Numbers	Query Attribute	Compare Attribute	CLEVR Humans
Human (Johnson et al., 2017b)	92.6	86.7	96.6	86.5	95.0	96.0	-
Q-type baseline (Johnson et al., 2017b)	41.8	34.6	50.2	51.0	36.0	51.3	-
LSTM (Johnson et al., 2017b)	46.8	41.7	61.1	69.8	36.8	51.8	36.5
CNN+LSTM (Johnson et al., 2017b)	52.3	43.7	65.2	67.1	49.3	53.0	43.2
CNN+LSTM+SA+MLP (Johnson et al., 2017a)	73.2	59.7	77.9	75.1	80.9	70.8	57.6
N2NMN* (Hu et al., 2017)	83.7	68.5	85.7	84.9	90.0	88.7	-
PG+EE (700K prog.)* (Johnson et al., 2017b)	96.9	92.7	97.1	98.7	98.1	98.9	-
CNN+LSTM+RN[‡] (Santoro et al., 2017)	95.5	90.1	97.8	93.6	97.9	97.1	-
CNN+GRU+FiLM (Perez et al., 2017)	97.7	94.3	99.1	96.8	99.1	99.1	75.9
MAC (Hudson and Manning, 2018)	98.9	97.1	99.5	99.1	99.5	99.5	81.5
TbD (Mascharka et al., 2018)	99.1	97.6	99.2	99.4	99.5	99.6	-
Stack-NMN (9 mod.)[†] (Hu et al., 2018)	91.41	81.78	95.78	85.23	95.45	95.68	68.06
LNMN (9 modules)	89.88	84.28	93.74	89.63	89.64	94.84	66.35
LNMN (11 modules)	90.52	84.91	95.21	91.06	90.03	94.97	65.68
LNMN (14 modules)	90.42	84.79	95.52	90.52	89.73	95.26	65.86

Table 1: CLEVR and CLEVR-Humans Accuracy by baseline methods and our models. (*) denotes use of extra supervision through program labels. ([‡]) denotes training from raw pixels. [†] Accuracy figures for our implementation of Stack-NMN.

Model	Overall	Count	Exist	Compare number	Query attribute	Compare Attribute
Original setting ($T = 5, L = 5, \text{map\_dim} = 384$)	89.78	84.54	93.46	88.70	89.59	94.87
Use hard-max for operation weights (for inference only) ($T = 5, L = 5, \text{map\_dim} = 384$)	87.99	81.53	94.11	87.70	88.27	91.55
$T = 9, L = 9, \text{map\_dim} = 256$	89.96	84.03	93.45	89.98	90.75	93.10
Concatenate all inputs followed by conv. layer	47.03	42.5	61.15	68.64	38.06	49.43

Table 2: Model Ablations for LNMN (CLEVR Validation set performance). The term 'map_dim' refers to the dimension of feature representation obtained at the input or output of each node of cell.

Model	Attn. modules (3 input)	Attn. modules (4 input)	Ans. modules (3 input)	Ans. modules (4 input)
LNMN (9)	4	2	1	1
LNMN (11)	4	2	2	2
LNMN (14)	5	4	2	2

Table 3: Number of modules of each type for different model ablations.

Model	VQA v2	VQA v1
Stack-NMN	58.23	59.84
LNMN (9 modules)	54.85	57.67

Table 4: Test Accuracy on Natural Image VQA datasets

over all examples) is defined as:

$$\text{IG}(\alpha_i^m) = \sum_{j=1}^{N} \sum_{k=1}^{p} \left[(\alpha_i^{m,k} - (\alpha_i^{m,k})') \times \right.$$

$$\left. \int_{\xi=0}^{1} \frac{\partial F(\mathcal{I}_j, \boldsymbol{q}_j, (1 - \xi) \times (\alpha_i^{m,k})' + \xi \times \alpha_i^{m,k})}{\partial \alpha_i^{m,k}} \right]$$

Please note that attributions are defined relative to an uninformative input called the baseline. We use a vector of all zeros as the baseline (denoted by $(\alpha_i^{m,k})'$). Table 5 shows the results for this experiment.

The module structure parameters (α parameters) of the *Answer* modules have their attributions to the final probability around 1-2 orders of magnitudes higher than rest of the modules. The higher influence of Answer modules can be explained by the fact that they receive the memory features from the previous time-step and the classifier receives the memory features of the final time-step. The job of *Attention* modules is to utilize intermediate

Module ID	Module type	min	max	sum	product	choose_1	choose_2
0	Attn. (3 input)	6.3 e4	2.7 e4	3.6 e4	1.1 e5	5.1 e4	1.6 e4
1	Attn. (3 input)	4.4 e4	1.8 e4	6.2 e4	1.4 e4	2.8 e4	1.7 e5
2	Attn. (3 input)	7.0 e4	3.3 e4	3.8 e4	1.1 e5	5.2 e4	1.5 e4
3	Attn. (3 input)	8.6 e3	6.2 e4	1.7 e4	1.8 e4	4.7 e4	3.0 e4
4	Attn. (4 input)	4.5 e4	3.2 e4	7.6 e4	1.7 e4	3.6 e4	2.1 e5
5	Attn. (4 input)	1.1 e5	5.6 e5	2.3 e5	8.5 e3	2.8 e4	1.8 e5
6	Ans. (3 input)	2.1 e6	4.3 e6	4.4 e6	8.3 e6	2.3 e6	4.9 e5
7	Ans. (4 input)	1.2 e5	5.8 e4	1.7 e5	5.2 e3	1.0 e5	4.5 e5

Table 5: Analysis of gradient attributions of α parameters corresponding to each module (LNMN (9 modules)), summed across all examples of CLEVR validation set.

attention maps to produce new feature maps which are used as input by the *Answer* modules.

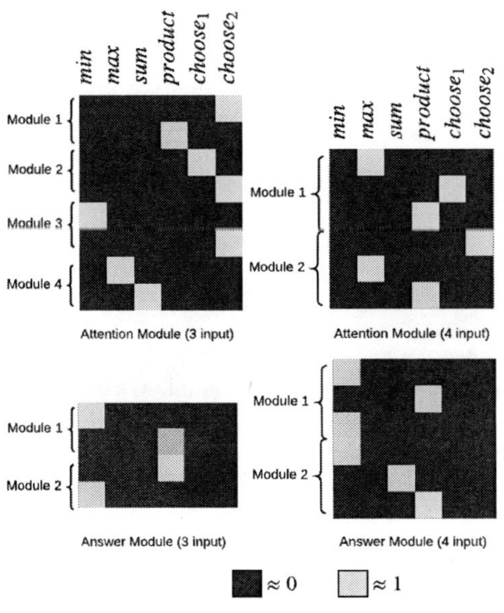

Figure 3: Visualization of module structure parameters (LNMN (11 modules)). For each module, each row denotes the $\alpha' = \sigma(\alpha)$ parameters of the corresponding node.

4.3 Visualization of module network parameters

In order to better interpret the individual contributions from each of the arithmetic operators to the modules, we plot them as color-maps for each type of module. The resulting visualizations are shown in Figure 3 for LNMN (11 modules). It is clear from the figure that the operation weights (or α' parameter) are approximately one-hot for each node. This is necessary in order to learn modules which act as composition of elementary operators on input feature maps rather than a mixture of operations at each node. The corresponding visualizations for LNMN (9 modules) and LNMN (14 modules) are given in Figure 8 and Figure 9 respectively (all of which are given in the Appendix A.3). The analytical expressions of modules learned by LNMN (11 modules) are shown in Table 6. The diversity of modules as given in their equations indicates that distinct modules emerge from training.

4.4 Measuring the role of individual arithmetic operators

Each module (*aka* cell) contains nodes which involves use of six elementary arithmetic operations (i.e. *min*, *max*, *sum*, *product*, *choose_1* and *choose_2*). We zero out the contribution to the node output for one of the arithmetic operations for all nodes in all modules and observe the degradation in the CLEVR validation accuracy[4]. The results of this study are shown in Table 7. The trend of overall accuracy shows that removing *max* and *product* operators results in maximum drop in overall accuracy ($\sim 50\%$). Other operators like *min*, *sum* and *choose_1* result in minimal drop in overall accuracy.

5 Related Work

Neural Architecture Search: Neural Architecture Search (NAS) is a technique to automatically learn the structure and connectivity of neural networks rather than training human-designed architectures. In (Zoph and Le, 2016), a recurrent neural network (RNN) based controller is used to predict the hyper-parameters of a CNN such as number of filters, stride, kernel size etc. They used RE-INFORCE (Williams, 1992) to train the controller

---

[4]The CLEVR test set ground truth answers are not public, so we use the validation set instead. However, Table 1 shows results for CLEVR test set (evaluated by the authors of CLEVR dataset).

Module type	Module implementation
Attention (3 inputs)	$O(img, a, c_{txt}) = conv_2(choose_2(conv_1(\mathcal{I}), a) \odot W_1 c_{txt}) = conv_2(a \odot W_1 c_{txt})$ $O(img, a, c_{txt}) = conv_2(choose_2(choose_1(conv_1(\mathcal{I}), a), W_1 c_{txt})) = conv_2(W_1 c_{txt})$ $O(img, a, c_{txt}) = conv_2(choose_2(min(conv_1(\mathcal{I}), a), W_1 c_{txt})) = conv_2(W_1 c_{txt})$ $O(img, a, c_{txt}) = conv_2(max(conv_1(\mathcal{I}), a) + W_1 c_{txt}))$
Attention (4 inputs)	$O(img, a_1, a_2, c_{txt}) = conv_2(choose_1(max(a_1, a_2), conv_1(\mathcal{I})) \odot W_1 c_{txt}))$ $\quad = conv_2(max(a_1, a_2) \odot W_1 c_{txt})$ $O(img, a_1, a_2, c_{txt}) = conv_2(max(choose_2(a_1, a_2), conv_1(\mathcal{I})) \odot W_1 c_{txt}))$ $\quad = conv_2(max(a_2, conv_1(\mathcal{I})) \odot W_1 c_{txt}))$
Answer (3 inputs)	$O(img, a, c_{txt}) = W_2[\sum min(conv_1(\mathcal{I}), a) \odot W_1 c_{txt}, W_1 c_{txt}, f_{mem}]$ $O(img, a, c_{txt}) = W_2[\sum min((conv_1(\mathcal{I}) \odot a), W_1 c_{txt}), W_1 c_{txt}, f_{mem}]$
Answer (4 inputs)	$O(img, a_1, a_2, c_{txt}) = W_2[\sum min((min(a_1, a_2) \odot conv_1(\mathcal{I})), W_1 c_{txt}), W_1 c_{txt}, f_{mem}]$ $O(img, a_1, a_2, c_{txt}) = W_2[\sum ((min(a_1, a_2) + conv_1(\mathcal{I})) \odot W_1 c_{txt}), W_1 c_{txt}, f_{mem}]$

Table 6: Analytical expression of modules learned by LNMN (11 modules). In the above equations, $\sum$ denotes sum over spatial dimensions of the feature tensor.

Operator Name	Overall	Count	Exist	Compare number	Query attribute	Compare Attribute
min	86.64	77.98	86.79	87.89	88.77	93.10
max	45.54	35.92	55.25	63.66	40.52	51.83
sum	82.67	69.89	80.25	85.22	87.69	90.05
product	34.65	14.55	51.49	48.79	30.31	49.92
choose_1	89.74	84.24	93.81	89.02	89.59	94.67
choose_2	79.45	64.77	76.07	82.96	86.78	84.94
Original Model	89.88	84.28	93.74	89.63	89.64	94.84

Table 7: Analysis of performance drop with removing operators from a trained model (LNMN 9 modules) on CLEVR validation set.

with validation set accuracy as the reward signal. As an alternative to reinforcement learning, evolutionary algorithms (Stanley, 2017) have been used to perform architecture search in (Real et al., 2017; Miikkulainen et al., 2019; Liu et al., 2017; Real et al., 2018). Recently, (Liu et al., 2018) proposed DARTS, a differentiable approach to perform architecture search and reported success in discovering high-performance architectures for both image classification and language modeling. Our approach for learning the structure of modules is inspired by DARTS. (Kirsch et al., 2018) proposes an EM style algorithm to learn black-box modules and their layout for image recognition and language modeling tasks.

Visual Reasoning Models: Among the end-to-end models for the task of visual reasoning, FiLM (Perez et al., 2017) uses Conditional Batch Normalization (CBN) (De Vries et al., 2017; Dumoulin et al., 2017) to modulate the channels of input convolutional features in a residual block. (Hudson and Manning, 2018) obtains the features by iteratively applying a Memory-Attention-Control (MAC) cell that learns to retrieve information from the image and aggregate the results into a recurrent memory.

(Santoro et al., 2017) constructs the feature representation by taking into account the relational interactions between objects of the image. With regards to the modular approaches, (Andreas et al., 2016b) proposes to compose neural network modules (with shared parameters) for each input question based on layout predicted by syntactic parse of the question. (Andreas et al., 2016a) extends this approach to question-answering in a database domain. In End-to-end Neural Module Networks (Hu et al., 2017), the layout prediction is relaxed by learning a layout policy with a sequence-to-sequence RNN. This layout policy is jointly trained along with the parameters of modules. The Stack-NMN (Hu et al., 2018) model is a differentiable version of End-to-end Neural Module Networks and we use this as our baseline model. In (Johnson et al., 2017b), the modules are residual blocks (convolutional), they learn the program generator separately and then fine-tune it along with the modules. TbD-net (Mascharka et al., 2018) builds upon the End-to-End Module Networks (Hu et al., 2017) but makes an important change in that the proposed modules explicitly utilize attention maps passed as inputs instead of learning whether or not to use them. This results in more interpretability of the modules since they perform specific functions.

Visual Question Answering: Visual question answering requires a learning model to answer sophisticated queries about visual inputs. Significant progress has been made in this direction to design neural networks that can answer queries about images. This can be attributed to the availability of relevant datasets which capture real-life images like DAQUAR (Malinowski and Fritz, 2014), COCO-QA (Ren et al., 2015a) and most recently VQA (v1 (Antol et al., 2015) and v2 (Goyal et al., 2017)). The most common approaches (Ren et al., 2015b; Noh et al., 2016) to this problem include construction of a joint embedding of question and image and treating it as a classification problem over the most frequent set of answers. Recent works (Jabri et al., 2016; Johnson et al., 2017a) have shown that the neural networks tend to exploit biases in the datasets without learning how to reason.

6   Conclusion

We have presented a differentiable approach to learn the modules needed in a visual reasoning task automatically. With this approach, we obtain results comparable to an analogous model in which modules are hand-specified for a particular visual reasoning task. In addition, we present an extensive analysis of the degree to which each module influences the prediction function of the model, the effect of each arithmetic operation on overall accuracy and the analytical expressions of the learned modules. In the future, we would like to benchmark this generic learnable neural module network with various other visual reasoning and visual question answering tasks.

References

Jacob Andreas, Marcus Rohrbach, Trevor Darrell, and Dan Klein. 2016a. Learning to compose neural networks for question answering. *arXiv preprint arXiv:1601.01705*.

Jacob Andreas, Marcus Rohrbach, Trevor Darrell, and Dan Klein. 2016b. Neural module networks. In *Proceedings of the IEEE Conference on Computer Vision and Pattern Recognition*, pages 39–48.

Stanislaw Antol, Aishwarya Agrawal, Jiasen Lu, Margaret Mitchell, Dhruv Batra, C. Lawrence Zitnick, and Devi Parikh. 2015. VQA: Visual Question Answering. In *International Conference on Computer Vision (ICCV)*.

Harm De Vries, Florian Strub, Jérémie Mary, Hugo Larochelle, Olivier Pietquin, and Aaron C Courville. 2017. Modulating early visual processing by language. In *Advances in Neural Information Processing Systems*, pages 6594–6604.

Vincent Dumoulin, Jonathon Shlens, and Manjunath Kudlur. 2017. A learned representation for artistic style. *Proc. of ICLR*.

Yash Goyal, Tejas Khot, Douglas Summers-Stay, Dhruv Batra, and Devi Parikh. 2017. Making the V in VQA matter: Elevating the role of image understanding in Visual Question Answering. In *Conference on Computer Vision and Pattern Recognition (CVPR)*.

Sepp Hochreiter and Jürgen Schmidhuber. 1997. Long short-term memory. *Neural computation*, 9(8):1735–1780.

Ronghang Hu, Jacob Andreas, Trevor Darrell, and Kate Saenko. 2018. Explainable neural computation via stack neural module networks. In *Proceedings of the European Conference on Computer Vision (ECCV)*, pages 53–69.

Ronghang Hu, Jacob Andreas, Marcus Rohrbach, Trevor Darrell, and Kate Saenko. 2017. Learning to reason: End-to-end module networks for visual question answering. *CoRR, abs/1704.05526*, 3.

Drew A Hudson and Christopher D Manning. 2018. Compositional attention networks for machine reasoning. *arXiv preprint arXiv:1803.03067*.

Niall Hurley and Scott Rickard. 2009. Comparing measures of sparsity. *IEEE Transactions on Information Theory*, 55(10):4723–4741.

Allan Jabri, Armand Joulin, and Laurens van der Maaten. 2016. Revisiting visual question answering baselines. In *European conference on computer vision*, pages 727–739. Springer.

Justin Johnson, Bharath Hariharan, Laurens van der Maaten, Li Fei-Fei, C Lawrence Zitnick, and Ross Girshick. 2017a. Clevr: A diagnostic dataset for compositional language and elementary visual reasoning. In *Computer Vision and Pattern Recognition (CVPR), 2017 IEEE Conference on*, pages 1988–1997. IEEE.

Justin Johnson, Bharath Hariharan, Laurens van der Maaten, Judy Hoffman, Li Fei-Fei, C Lawrence Zitnick, and Ross Girshick. 2017b. Inferring and executing programs for visual reasoning. In *ICCV*.

Diederik P Kingma and Jimmy Ba. 2014. Adam: A method for stochastic optimization. *arXiv preprint arXiv:1412.6980*.

Louis Kirsch, Julius Kunze, and David Barber. 2018. Modular networks: Learning to decompose neural computation. In *Advances in Neural Information Processing Systems*, pages 2414–2423.

Hanxiao Liu, Karen Simonyan, Oriol Vinyals, Chrisantha Fernando, and Koray Kavukcuoglu. 2017. Hierarchical representations for efficient architecture search. *arXiv preprint arXiv:1711.00436*.

Hanxiao Liu, Karen Simonyan, and Yiming Yang. 2018. Darts: Differentiable architecture search. *arXiv preprint arXiv:1806.09055*.

Mateusz Malinowski and Mario Fritz. 2014. A multiworld approach to question answering about real-world scenes based on uncertain input. In *Advances in neural information processing systems*, pages 1682–1690.

David Mascharka, Philip Tran, Ryan Soklaski, and Arjun Majumdar. 2018. Transparency by design: Closing the gap between performance and interpretability in visual reasoning. *2018 IEEE/CVF Conference on Computer Vision and Pattern Recognition*, pages 4942–4950.

Risto Miikkulainen, Jason Liang, Elliot Meyerson, Aditya Rawal, Daniel Fink, Olivier Francon, Bala Raju, Hormoz Shahrzad, Arshak Navruzyan, Nigel Duffy, et al. 2019. Evolving deep neural networks. In *Artificial Intelligence in the Age of Neural Networks and Brain Computing*, pages 293–312. Elsevier.

Hyeonwoo Noh, Paul Hongsuck Seo, and Bohyung Han. 2016. Image question answering using convolutional neural network with dynamic parameter prediction. In *Proceedings of the IEEE conference on computer vision and pattern recognition*, pages 30–38.

Ethan Perez, Florian Strub, Harm de Vries, Vincent Dumoulin, and Aaron C. Courville. 2017. Film: Visual reasoning with a general conditioning layer. *CoRR*, abs/1709.07871.

Esteban Real, Alok Aggarwal, Yanping Huang, and Quoc V Le. 2018. Regularized evolution for image classifier architecture search. *arXiv preprint arXiv:1802.01548*.

Esteban Real, Sherry Moore, Andrew Selle, Saurabh Saxena, Yutaka Leon Suematsu, Jie Tan, Quoc Le, and Alex Kurakin. 2017. Large-scale evolution of image classifiers. *arXiv preprint arXiv:1703.01041*.

Mengye Ren, Ryan Kiros, and Richard Zemel. 2015a. Exploring models and data for image question answering. In *Advances in neural information processing systems*, pages 2953–2961.

Mengye Ren, Ryan Kiros, and Richard Zemel. 2015b. Image question answering: A visual semantic embedding model and a new dataset. *Proc. Advances in Neural Inf. Process. Syst*, 1(2):5.

Anna Rohrbach, Marcus Rohrbach, Ronghang Hu, Trevor Darrell, and Bernt Schiele. 2016. Grounding of textual phrases in images by reconstruction. In *European Conference on Computer Vision*, pages 817–834. Springer.

Adam Santoro, David Raposo, David G Barrett, Mateusz Malinowski, Razvan Pascanu, Peter Battaglia, and Timothy Lillicrap. 2017. A simple neural network module for relational reasoning. In *Advances in neural information processing systems*, pages 4967–4976.

Kenneth O Stanley. 2017. Neuroevolution: A different kind of deep learning.

Mukund Sundararajan, Ankur Taly, and Qiqi Yan. 2017. Axiomatic attribution for deep networks. *arXiv preprint arXiv:1703.01365*.

Ronald J Williams. 1992. Simple statistical gradient-following algorithms for connectionist reinforcement learning. *Machine learning*, 8(3-4):229–256.

Barret Zoph and Quoc V Le. 2016. Neural architecture search with reinforcement learning. *arXiv preprint arXiv:1611.01578*.

Aligning Multilingual Word Embeddings for Cross-Modal Retrieval Task

Alireza Mohammadshahi
IDIAP Research Inst.
EPFL
alireza.mohammadshahi@epfl.ch

Rémi Lebret
EPFL
remi.lebret@epfl.ch

Karl Aberer
EPFL
karl.aberer@epfl.ch

Abstract

In this paper, we propose a new approach to learn multimodal multilingual embeddings for matching images and their relevant captions in two languages. We combine two existing objective functions to make images and captions close in a joint embedding space while adapting the alignment of word embeddings between existing languages in our model. We show that our approach enables better generalization, achieving state-of-the-art performance in text-to-image and image-to-text retrieval task, and caption-caption similarity task. Two multimodal multilingual datasets are used for evaluation: Multi30k with German and English captions and Microsoft-COCO with English and Japanese captions.

1 Introduction

In recent years, there has been a huge and significant amount of research in text and image retrieval tasks which needs the joint modeling of both modalities. Further, a large number of image-text datasets have become available (Elliott et al., 2016; Hodosh et al., 2013; Young et al., 2014; Lin et al., 2014), and several models have been proposed to generate captions for images in the dataset (Lu et al., 2018; Bernardi et al., 2016; Anderson et al., 2017; Lu et al., 2016; Mao et al., 2014; Rennie et al., 2016). There has been a great amount of research in learning a joint embedding space for texts and images in order to use the model in sentence-based image search or cross-modal retrieval task (Frome et al., 2013; Kiros et al., 2014; Donahue et al., 2014; Lazaridou et al., 2015; Socher et al., 2013; Hodosh et al., 2013; Karpathy et al., 2014).

Previous works in image-caption task and learning a joint embedding space for texts and images are mostly related to English language, however, recently there is a large amount of research in other languages due to the availability of multilingual datasets (Funaki and Nakayama, 2015; Elliott et al., 2016; Rajendran et al., 2015; Miyazaki and Shimizu, 2016; Lucia Specia and Elliott, 2016; Young et al., 2014; Hitschler and Riezler, 2016; Yoshikawa et al., 2017). The aim of these models is to map images and their captions in a single language into a joint embedding space (Rajendran et al., 2015; Calixto et al., 2017).

Related to our work, Gella et al. (2017) proposed a model to learn a multilingual multimodal embedding by utilizing an image as a pivot between languages of captions. While a text encoder is trained for each language in Gella et al. (2017), we propose instead a model that learns a shared and language-independent text encoder between languages, yielding better generalization. It is generally important to adapt word embeddings for the task at hand. Our model enables tuning of word embeddings while keeping the two languages aligned during training, building a task-specific shared embedding space for existing languages.

In this attempt, we define a new objective function that combines a pairwise ranking loss with a loss that maintains the alignment in multiple languages. For the latter, we use the objective function proposed in Joulin et al. (2018) for learning a linear mapping between languages inspired by cross-domain similarity local scaling (CSLS) retrieval criterion (Conneau et al., 2017) which obtains the state-of-the-art performance on word translation task.

In the next sections, the proposed approach is called Aligning Multilingual Embeddings for cross-modal retrieval (AME). With experiments on two multimodal multilingual datasets, we show that AME outperforms existing models on text-image multimodal retrieval tasks. The code we used to train and evaluate the model is available at `https://github.com/alirezamshi/AME-CMR`

Proceedings of the Beyond Vision and LANguage: inTEgrating Real-world kNowledge (LANTERN), pages 11–17
Hong Kong, China, November 3, 2019. ©2019 Association for Computational Linguistics

2 Datasets

We use two multilingual image-caption datasets to evaluate our model, Multi30k and Microsoft COCO (Elliott et al., 2016; Lin et al., 2014).

Multi30K is a dataset with 31'014 German translations of English captions and 155'070 independently collected German and English captions. In this paper, we use independently collected captions which each image contains five German and five English captions. The training set includes 29'000 images. The validation and test sets contain 1'000 images.

MS-COCO (Lin et al., 2014) contains 123'287 images and five English captions per image. Yoshikawa et al. (2017) proposed a model which generates Japanese descriptions for images. We divide the dataset based on Karpathy and Li (2014). The training set contains 113'287 images. Each validation and test set contains 5'000 images.

3 Problem Formulation

3.1 Model for Learning a Multilingual Multimodal Representation

Assume image i and captions c_{X_i} and c_{Y_i} are given in two languages, X and Y respectively. Our aim is to learn a model where the image i and its captions c_{X_i} and c_{Y_i} are close in a joint embedding space of dimension m. AME consists of two encoders f_i and f_c, which encode images and captions. As multilingual text encoder, we use a recurrent neural network with gated recurrent unit (GRU). For the image encoder, we use a convolutional neural network (CNN) architecture. The similarity between a caption c and an image i in the joint embedding space is measured with a similarity function $P(c, i)$. The objective function is as follows (inspired by Gella et al. (2017)):

$$L_R = \sum_{(c_{S_i}, i)} \Big(\sum_{c_{S_j}} max\{0, \alpha - P(c_{S_i}, i) + P(c_{S_j}, i)\} + \sum_j max\{0, \alpha - P(c_{S_i}, i) + P(c_{S_i}, j)\}\Big) \quad (1)$$

Where S stands for both languages, and α is the margin. c_{S_j} and j are irrelevant caption and image of the gold-standard pair (c_{S_i}, i).

3.2 Alignment Model

Each word k in the language X is defined by a word embedding $x_k \in \mathbb{R}^d$ ($y_k \in \mathbb{R}^d$ in the language Y respectively). Given a bilingual lexicon of N pairs of words, we assume the first n pairs $\{(x_i, y_i)\}_{i=1}^n$ are the initial seeds, and our aim is to augment it to all word pairs that are not in the initial lexicons. Mikolov et al. (2013) proposed a model to learn a linear mapping $W \in \mathbb{R}^{d \times d}$ between the source and target languages:

$$min_{W \in \mathbb{R}^{d \times d}} \frac{1}{n} \sum_{i=1}^n \ell(W x_i, y_i | x_i, y_i) \quad (2)$$
$$\ell(W x_i, y_i | x_i, y_i) = (W x_i - y_i)^2$$

Where ℓ is a square loss. One can find the translation of a source word in the target language by performing a nearest neighbor search with Euclidean distance. But, the model suffers from a "hubness problem": some word embeddings become uncommonly the nearest neighbors of a great number of other words (Doddington et al., 1998; Dinu and Baroni, 2014).

In order to resolve this issue, Joulin et al. (2018) proposed a new objective function inspired by CSLS criterion to learn the linear mapping:

$$L_A = \frac{1}{n} \sum_{i=1}^n -2x_i^T W^T y_i + \frac{1}{k} \sum_{y_j \in \mathcal{N}_Y(W x_i)} x_i^T W^T y_j + \frac{1}{k} \sum_{W x_j \in \mathcal{N}_X(y_i)} x_j^T W^T y_i \quad (3)$$

Where $\mathcal{N}_X(y_i)$ means the k-nearest neighbors of y_i in the set of source language X. They constrained the linear mapping W to be orthogonal, and word vectors are $l2$-normalized.

The whole loss function is the equally weighted summation of the aforementioned objective functions:

$$L_{total} = L_R + L_A \quad (4)$$

The model architecture is illustrated in Figure 1. We observe that updating the parameters in (3) every T iterations with learning rate lr_{align} obtains the best performance.

We use two different similarity functions, symmetric and asymmetric. For the former, we use the cosine similarity function and for the latter, we use the metric proposed in Vendrov et al. (2015), which encodes the partial order structure of the visual-semantic hierarchy. The metric similarity is defined as:

$$S(a, b) = -||max(0, b - a)||^2 \quad (5)$$

Where a and b are the embeddings of image and caption.

	Image to Text				Text to Image				
	R@1	R@5	R@10	Mr	R@1	R@5	R@10	Mr	Alignment
symmetric									
Parallel (Gella et al., 2017)	31.7	62.4	74.1	3	24.7	53.9	65.7	5	-
UVS (Kiros et al., 2014)	23.0	50.7	62.9	5	16.8	42.0	56.5	8	-
EmbeddingNet (Wang et al., 2017)	40.7	69.7	79.2	-	29.2	59.6	71.7	-	-
sm-LSTM (Huang et al., 2016)	42.5	71.9	81.5	2	30.2	60.4	72.3	3	-
VSE++ (Faghri et al., 2017)	**43.7**	71.9	82.1	2	32.3	60.9	72.1	3	-
Mono	41.4	74.2	84.2	2	32.1	63.0	73.9	3	-
FME	39.2	71.1	82.1	2	29.7	62.5	74.1	3	76.81%
AME	43.5	**77.2**	**85.3**	**2**	**34.0**	**64.2**	**75.4**	**3**	66.91%
asymmetric									
Pivot (Gella et al., 2017)	33.8	62.8	75.2	3	26.2	56.4	68.4	4	-
Parallel (Gella et al., 2017)	31.5	61.4	74.7	3	27.1	56.2	66.9	4	-
Mono	47.7	77.1	86.9	2	35.8	66.6	76.8	3	-
FME	44.9	76.9	86.4	2	34.2	66.1	77.1	3	76.81%
AME	**50.5**	**79.7**	**88.4**	**1**	**38.0**	**68.5**	**78.4**	**2**	73.10%

Table 1: Image-caption ranking results for English (Multi30k)

	Image to Text				Text to Image				
	R@1	R@5	R@10	Mr	R@1	R@5	R@10	Mr	Alignment
symmetric									
Parallel (Gella et al., 2017)	28.2	57.7	71.3	4	20.9	46.9	59.3	6	-
Mono	34.2	67.5	79.6	3	26.5	54.7	66.2	4	-
FME	36.8	69.4	80.8	2	26.6	56.2	68.5	4	76.81%
AME	**39.6**	**72.7**	**82.7**	**2**	**28.9**	**58.0**	**68.7**	**4**	66.91%
asymmetric									
Pivot (Gella et al., 2017)	28.2	61.9	73.4	3	22.5	49.3	61.7	6	-
Parallel (Gella et al., 2017)	30.2	60.4	72.8	3	21.8	50.5	62.3	5	-
Mono	**42.0**	72.5	83.0	2	29.6	58.4	69.6	4	-
FME	40.5	73.3	83.4	2	29.6	59.2	**72.1**	3	76.81%
AME	40.5	**74.3**	**83.4**	**2**	**31.0**	**60.5**	70.6	**3**	73.10%

Table 2: Image-caption ranking results for German (Multi30k)

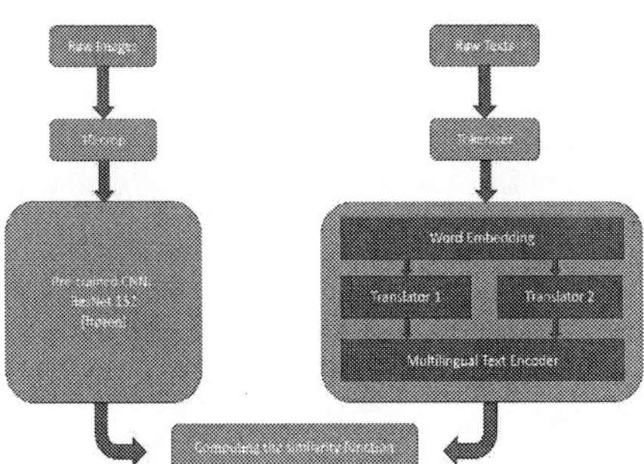

Figure 1: The AME - model architecture

4 Experiment and Results

4.1 Details of Implementation [1]

We use a mini-batch of size 128. We use Adam optimizer with learning rate 0.00011 (0.00006) and with early stopping on the validation set. We set the dimensionality of joint embedding space and the GRU hidden layer to $m = 1024$. We utilize the pre-trained aligned word vectors of FastText for the initial word embeddings. For Japanese word embedding, we use pre-trained word vectors of FastText[2], then align it to the English word embedding with the same hyper-parameters used for MS-COCO. We set the margin $\alpha = 0.2$ and $\alpha = 0.05$ for symmetric and asymmetric similarity functions respectively.

We assign k-nearest neighbors to be 5 (4). We set $T = 500$, and $lr_{align} = 2$ (5). We tokenize English and German captions with Europarl tokenizer (Koehn, 2005). For the Japanese caption, we use Mecab analyzer (Kudo et al., 2004). We train the model for 30 (20) epochs with updating the learning rate (divided by 10) on epoch 15 (10).

To extract features of images, we use a ResNet152 (He et al., 2015) CNN architecture pre-trained on Imagenet and extract the image features from FC7, the penultimate fully connected layer. We use average features from 10-crop of the re-scaled images.

For the metric of alignment, we use bilingual lexicons of Multilingual Unsupervised and Super-

---

[1] In this section, the hyper-parameters in parentheses are related to the model trained on MS-COCO.

[2] Available at `https://fasttext.cc/docs/en/crawl-vectors.html`, and `https://fasttext.cc/docs/en/aligned-vectors.html`.

	Image to Text				Text to Image				
	R@1	R@5	R@10	Mr	R@1	R@5	R@10	Mr	Alignment
symmetric									
UVS (Kiros et al., 2014)	43.4	75.7	85.8	2	31.0	66.7	79.9	3	-
EmbeddingNet (Wang et al., 2017)	50.4	79.3	89.4	-	39.8	75.3	86.6	-	-
sm-LSTM (Huang et al., 2016)	53.2	83.1	91.5	1	40.7	75.8	87.4	2	-
VSE++ (Faghri et al., 2017)	**58.3**	**86.1**	93.3	1	**43.6**	77.6	87.8	2	-
Mono	51.8	84.8	93.5	1	40.0	77.3	89.4	2	-
FME	42.2	76.6	91.1	2	31.2	69.2	83.7	3	92.70%
AME	54.6	85	**94.3**	**1**	42.1	**78.7**	**90.3**	**2**	82.54%
asymmetric									
Mono	53.2	87.0	94.7	1	42.3	78.9	90	2	-
FME	48.3	83.6	93.6	2	37.2	75.4	88.4	2	92.70%
AME	**58.8**	**88.6**	**96.2**	**1**	**46.2**	**82.5**	**91.9**	**2**	84.99%

Table 3: Image-caption ranking results for English (MS-COCO)

	Image to Text				Text to Image				
	R@1	R@5	R@10	Mr	R@1	R@5	R@10	Mr	Alignment
symmetric									
Mono	42.7	77.7	88.5	2	33.1	69.8	84.3	3	-
FME	40.7	77.7	88.3	2	30.0	68.9	83.1	3	92.70%
AME	**50.2**	**85.6**	**93.1**	**1**	**40.2**	**76.7**	**87.8**	**2**	82.54%
asymmetric									
Mono	49.9	83.4	93.7	2	39.7	76.5	88.3	**2**	-
FME	48.8	81.9	91.9	2	37.0	74.8	87.0	**2**	92.70%
AME	**55.5**	**87.9**	**95.2**	**1**	**44.9**	**80.7**	**89.3**	**2**	84.99%

Table 4: Image-caption ranking results for Japanese (MS-COCO)

	EN → DE			DE → EN		
	R@1	R@5	R@10	R@1	R@5	R@10
FME	51.4	76.4	84.5	46.9	71.2	79.1
AME	**51.7**	**76.7**	**85.1**	**49.1**	**72.6**	**80.5**

Table 5: Textual similarity scores (asymmetric, Multi30k).

vised Embeddings (MUSE) benchmark (Lample et al., 2017). MUSE is a large-scale high-quality bilingual dictionaries for training and evaluating the translation task. We extract the training words of descriptions in two languages. For training, we combine "full" and "test" sections of MUSE, then filter them to the training words. For evaluation, we filter "train" section of MUSE to the training words. [3]

For evaluating the benefit of the proposed objective function, we compare AME with monolingual training (Mono), and multilingual training without the alignment model described in Section 3.2. For the latter, the pre-aligned word embeddings are frozen during training (FME). We add Mono since the proposed model in Gella et al. (2017) did not utilize pre-trained word embeddings for the initialization, and the image encoder is different (ResNet152 vs. VGG19).

We compare models based on two retrieval metrics, recall at position k (R@k) and Median of ranks (Mr).

4.2 Multi30k Results

In Table 1 and 2, we show the results for English and German captions. For English captions, we see 21.28% improvement on average compared to Kiros et al. (2014). There is a 1.8% boost on average compared to Mono due to more training data and multilingual text encoder. AME performs better than FME model on both symmetric and asymmetric modes, which shows the advantage of fine-tuning word embeddings during training. We have 25.26% boost on average compared to Kiros et al. (2014) in asymmetric mode.

For German descriptions, The results are 11.05% better on average compared to (Gella et al., 2017) in symmetric mode. AME also achieves competitive or better results than FME model in German descriptions too.

4.3 MS-COCO Results[4]

In Table 3 and 4, we show the performance of AME and baselines for English and Japanese captions. We achieve 10.42% improvement on aver-

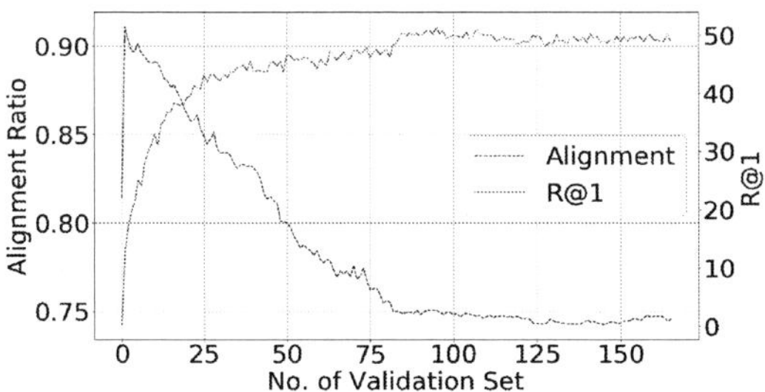

Figure 2: Alignment ratio in each validation step (asymmetric mode - image-to-text - Multi30k dataset)

age compared to Kiros et al. (2014) in the symmetric manner. We show that adapting the word embedding for the task at hand, boosts the general performance, since AME model significantly outperforms FME model in both languages.

For the Japanese captions, AME reaches 6.25% and 3.66% better results on average compared to monolingual model in symmetric and asymmetric modes, respectively.

4.4 Alignment results

In Tables 1 and 2, we can see that the alignment ratio for AME is 6.80% lower than FME which means that the translators can almost keep languages aligned in Multi30k dataset. In MS-COCO dataset, the alignment ratio for AME is 8.93% lower compared to FME.

We compute the alignment ratio and recall at position 1 (R@1) in each validation step. Figure 2 shows the trade-off between alignment and retrieval tasks. At the first few epochs, the model improves the alignment ratio since the retrieval task hasn't seen enough number of instances. Then, the retrieval task tries to fine-tune word embeddings. Finally, they reach an agreement near the half of training process. At this point, we update the learning rate of retrieval task to improve the performance, and the alignment ratio preserves constant.

Additionally, we also train AME model without adding the alignment objective function, and the model breaks the alignment between the initial aligned word embeddings, so it's essential to add the alignment objective function to the retrieval task.

4.5 Caption-Caption Similarity Scores

Given the caption in a language, the task is to retrieve the related caption in another language. In Table 5, we show the performance on Multi30k dataset in asymmetric mode. AME outperforms the FME model, confirming the importance of word embeddings adaptation.

5 Conclusion

We proposed a multimodal model with a shared multilingual text encoder by adapting the alignment between languages for image-description retrieval task while training. We introduced a loss function which is a combination of a pairwise ranking loss and a loss that maintains the alignment of word embeddings in multiple languages. Through experiments with different multimodal multilingual datasets, we have shown that our approach yields better generalization performance on image-to-text and text-to-image retrieval tasks, as well as caption-caption similarity task.

In the future work, we can investigate on applying self-attention models like Transformer (Vaswani et al., 2017) on the shared text encoder to find a more comprehensive representation for descriptions in the dataset. Additionally, we can explore the effect of a weighted summation of two loss functions instead of equally summing them together.

6 Acknowledgement

We gratefully acknowledge the support of NVIDIA Corporation with the donation of the Titan Xp GPU used for this research.

References

Peter Anderson, Xiaodong He, Chris Buehler, Damien Teney, Mark Johnson, Stephen Gould, and Lei Zhang. 2017. Bottom-up and top-down attention for image captioning and VQA. *CoRR*, abs/1707.07998.

Raffaella Bernardi, Ruket Çakici, Desmond Elliott, Aykut Erdem, Erkut Erdem, Nazli Ikizler-Cinbis, Frank Keller, Adrian Muscat, and Barbara Plank. 2016. Automatic description generation from images: A survey of models, datasets, and evaluation measures. *CoRR*, abs/1601.03896.

Iacer Calixto, Qun Liu, and Nick Campbell. 2017. Multilingual multi-modal embeddings for natural language processing. *CoRR*, abs/1702.01101.

Alexis Conneau, Guillaume Lample, Marc'Aurelio Ranzato, Ludovic Denoyer, and Hervé Jégou. 2017. Word translation without parallel data. *CoRR*, abs/1710.04087.

Georgiana Dinu and Marco Baroni. 2014. Improving zero-shot learning by mitigating the hubness problem. *CoRR*, abs/1412.6568.

George Doddington, Walter Liggett, Alvin Martin, Mark Przybocki, and Douglas Reynolds. 1998. Sheep, goats, lambs and wolves a statistical analysis of speaker performance in the nist 1998 speaker recognition evaluation. In *INTERNATIONAL CONFERENCE ON SPOKEN LANGUAGE PROCESSING*.

Jeff Donahue, Lisa Anne Hendricks, Sergio Guadarrama, Marcus Rohrbach, Subhashini Venugopalan, Kate Saenko, and Trevor Darrell. 2014. Long-term recurrent convolutional networks for visual recognition and description. *CoRR*, abs/1411.4389.

Desmond Elliott, Stella Frank, Khalil Sima'an, and Lucia Specia. 2016. Multi30k: Multilingual english-german image descriptions. *CoRR*, abs/1605.00459.

Fartash Faghri, David J. Fleet, Ryan Kiros, and Sanja Fidler. 2017. VSE++: improved visual-semantic embeddings. *CoRR*, abs/1707.05612.

Andrea Frome, Greg S Corrado, Jon Shlens, Samy Bengio, Jeff Dean, Marc Aurelio Ranzato, and Tomas Mikolov. 2013. Devise: A deep visual-semantic embedding model. In C. J. C. Burges, L. Bottou, M. Welling, Z. Ghahramani, and K. Q. Weinberger, editors, *Advances in Neural Information Processing Systems 26*, pages 2121–2129. Curran Associates, Inc.

Ruka Funaki and Hideki Nakayama. 2015. Image-mediated learning for zero-shot cross-lingual document retrieval. In *Proceedings of the 2015 Conference on Empirical Methods in Natural Language Processing*, pages 585–590. Association for Computational Linguistics.

Spandana Gella, Rico Sennrich, Frank Keller, and Mirella Lapata. 2017. Image pivoting for learning multilingual multimodal representations. *CoRR*, abs/1707.07601.

Kaiming He, Xiangyu Zhang, Shaoqing Ren, and Jian Sun. 2015. Deep residual learning for image recognition. *CoRR*, abs/1512.03385.

Julian Hitschler and Stefan Riezler. 2016. Multimodal pivots for image caption translation. *CoRR*, abs/1601.03916.

Micah Hodosh, Peter Young, and Julia Hockenmaier. 2013. Framing image description as a ranking task: Data, models and evaluation metrics. In *J. Artif. Intell. Res.*

Yan Huang, Wei Wang, and Liang Wang. 2016. Instance-aware image and sentence matching with selective multimodal LSTM. *CoRR*, abs/1611.05588.

Armand Joulin, Piotr Bojanowski, Tomas Mikolov, Hervé Jégou, and Edouard Grave. 2018. Loss in translation: Learning bilingual word mapping with a retrieval criterion. In *Proceedings of the 2018 Conference on Empirical Methods in Natural Language Processing*.

Andrej Karpathy, Armand Joulin, and Li F Fei-Fei. 2014. Deep fragment embeddings for bidirectional image sentence mapping. In Z. Ghahramani, M. Welling, C. Cortes, N. D. Lawrence, and K. Q. Weinberger, editors, *Advances in Neural Information Processing Systems 27*, pages 1889–1897. Curran Associates, Inc.

Andrej Karpathy and Fei-Fei Li. 2014. Deep visual-semantic alignments for generating image descriptions. *CoRR*, abs/1412.2306.

Ryan Kiros, Ruslan Salakhutdinov, and Richard S. Zemel. 2014. Unifying visual-semantic embeddings with multimodal neural language models. *CoRR*, abs/1411.2539.

Philipp Koehn. 2005. Europarl: A Parallel Corpus for Statistical Machine Translation. In *Conference Proceedings: the tenth Machine Translation Summit*, pages 79–86, Phuket, Thailand. AAMT, AAMT.

Taku Kudo, Kaoru Yamamoto, and Yuji Matsumoto. 2004. Applying conditional random fields to japanese morphological analysis. In *In Proc. of EMNLP*, pages 230–237.

Guillaume Lample, Ludovic Denoyer, and Marc'Aurelio Ranzato. 2017. Unsupervised machine translation using monolingual corpora only. *CoRR*, abs/1711.00043.

Angeliki Lazaridou, Nghia The Pham, and Marco Baroni. 2015. Combining language and vision with a multimodal skip-gram model. *CoRR*, abs/1501.02598.

Tsung-Yi Lin, Michael Maire, Serge J. Belongie, Lubomir D. Bourdev, Ross B. Girshick, James Hays, Pietro Perona, Deva Ramanan, Piotr Dollár, and C. Lawrence Zitnick. 2014. Microsoft COCO: common objects in context. *CoRR*, abs/1405.0312.

Jiasen Lu, Caiming Xiong, Devi Parikh, and Richard Socher. 2016. Knowing when to look: Adaptive attention via A visual sentinel for image captioning. *CoRR*, abs/1612.01887.

Jiasen Lu, Jianwei Yang, Dhruv Batra, and Devi Parikh. 2018. Neural baby talk. *CoRR*, abs/1803.09845.

Khalil Simaan Lucia Specia, Stella Frank and Desmond Elliott. 2016. A shared task on multimodal machine translation and cross-lingual image description.

Junhua Mao, Wei Xu, Yi Yang, Jiang Wang, and Alan L. Yuille. 2014. Deep captioning with multimodal recurrent neural networks (m-rnn). *CoRR*, abs/1412.6632.

Tomas Mikolov, Quoc V. Le, and Ilya Sutskever. 2013. Exploiting similarities among languages for machine translation. *CoRR*, abs/1309.4168.

Takashi Miyazaki and Nobuyuki Shimizu. 2016. Cross-lingual image caption generation. In *Proceedings of the 54th Annual Meeting of the Association for Computational Linguistics (Volume 1: Long Papers)*, pages 1780–1790. Association for Computational Linguistics.

Janarthanan Rajendran, Mitesh M. Khapra, Sarath Chandar, and Balaraman Ravindran. 2015. Bridge correlational neural networks for multilingual multimodal representation learning. *CoRR*, abs/1510.03519.

Steven J. Rennie, Etienne Marcheret, Youssef Mroueh, Jarret Ross, and Vaibhava Goel. 2016. Self-critical sequence training for image captioning. *CoRR*, abs/1612.00563.

Richard Socher, Andrej Karpathy, Quoc V. Le, Chris D. Manning, and Andrew Y. Ng. 2013. Grounded compositional semantics for finding and describing images with sentences. *Transactions of the Association for Computational Linguistics*.

Ashish Vaswani, Noam Shazeer, Niki Parmar, Jakob Uszkoreit, Llion Jones, Aidan N. Gomez, Lukasz Kaiser, and Illia Polosukhin. 2017. Attention is all you need.

Ivan Vendrov, Ryan Kiros, Sanja Fidler, and Raquel Urtasun. 2015. Order-embeddings of images and language. *CoRR*, abs/1511.06361.

Liwei Wang, Yin Li, and Svetlana Lazebnik. 2017. Learning two-branch neural networks for image-text matching tasks. *CoRR*, abs/1704.03470.

Yuya Yoshikawa, Yutaro Shigeto, and Akikazu Takeuchi. 2017. STAIR captions: Constructing a large-scale japanese image caption dataset. *CoRR*, abs/1705.00823.

Peter Young, Alice Lai, Micah Hodosh, and Julia Hockenmaier. 2014. From image descriptions to visual denotations. *Transactions of the Association for Computational Linguistics*, 2:67–78.

Big Generalizations with *Small* Data:
Exploring the Role of Training Samples in Learning Adjectives of Size

Sandro Pezzelle and **Raquel Fernández**
Institute for Logic, Language, and Computation
University of Amsterdam
{s.pezzelle|raquel.fernandez}@uva.nl

Abstract

In this paper, we experiment with a recently proposed visual reasoning task dealing with quantities – modeling the multimodal, contextually-dependent meaning of size adjectives ('big', 'small') – and explore the impact of varying the training data on the learning behavior of a state-of-art system. In previous work, models have been shown to fail in generalizing to *unseen* adjective-noun combinations. Here, we investigate whether, and to what extent, seeing some of these cases during training helps a model understand the rule subtending the task, i.e., that being *big* implies being *not small*, and vice versa. We show that relatively few examples are enough to understand this relationship, and that developing a specific, mutually exclusive representation of size adjectives is beneficial to the task.

1 Introduction

A recently proposed visual reasoning task challenges models to learn the meaning of *size* adjectives ('big', 'small') from visually-grounded contexts (MALeViC; Pezzelle and Fernández, 2019). Differently from standard approaches in language and vision treating size as a *fixed* attribute of objects (Johnson et al., 2017), in MALeViC what counts as 'big' or 'small' is defined *contextually*, based on a cognitively-motivated threshold function evaluating the size of all the *relevant* objects in a scene (Schmidt et al., 2009). In the most challenging version of the task, SET+POS, the subset of relevant objects (i.e., the reference set) comprises all the objects belonging to the same category as the queried one. Given a scene depicting a number of colored shapes (e.g., the leftmost image in Figure 1) and a sentence about one object's size (e.g., 'The white rectangle is a *big* rectangle'), models have to assess whether the sentence is *true* or *false* in that context; i.e., whether the white rectangle is *big* given the other rectangles in the scene.

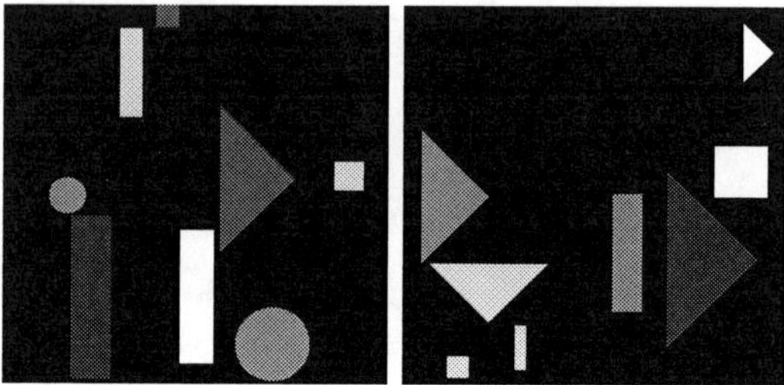

Figure 1: SET+POS. Two original (ORIG) examples. **Left (ORIG):** The white rectangle is a *big* rectangle, True. **Right (ORIG):** The blue triangle is a *small* triangle, False. To test model abilities in handling *unexpected* cases, an increasing number of ORIG training samples is modified by *swapping* both the size adjective and its ground-truth (SWAP). **Left (SWAP):** *small*, False. **Right (SWAP):** *big*, True. Best viewed in color.

Among the tested models, FiLM (Perez et al., 2018) turned out to be the best overall architecture for the task. However, when tested with adjective-noun combinations that were never *seen* in training (i.e., the model has been taught what means to be *big* for circles and rectangles or *small* for triangles and squares, but not, e.g., what means to be *small* for a circle), FiLM was shown to use a default strategy which ignores the adjective rather than applying it *compositionally*. This finding is in line with previous evidence showing the lack of compositionality in neural networks (Baroni, 2019), either in multimodal tasks like visual question answering (Agrawal et al., 2017) and visual reasoning (Johnson et al., 2017), or when coping with language data (Lake and Baroni, 2018; Loula et al., 2018). To solve this well-known issue, several attempts have been made to develop new models and techniques (Agrawal et al., 2018; Ramakrishnan et al., 2018; Korrel et al., 2019), and several datasets have been proposed to test compositional abilities of systems (Agrawal et al., 2017, 2018).

Proceedings of the Beyond Vision and LANguage: inTEgrating Real-world kNowledge (LANTERN), pages 18–23
Hong Kong, China, November 3, 2019. ©2019 Association for Computational Linguistics

In this work, we focus on a tightly related problem, that is, generalization with little data. Since models do not learn an *abstract* representation of 'big' and 'small' that can be applied compositionally to *unseen* examples, we test whether, and to what extent, this problem can be alleviated by seeing some of these 'unseen' cases during training. We refer to these cases as *unexpected* (due to their low frequency compared to the more frequent, *expected* ones), and test whether injecting an increasing proportion of these examples in the training data helps models understand the rule subtending the task, i.e., that being *big* implies being *not small*, and vice versa. Intuitively, the model could (1) stick to the default strategy and correctly predict only the *expected* examples, or (2) learn a more general rule that also accounts for the *unexpected* cases. Here, we are interested in checking how much data is required to start adopting the latter strategy, and aim to understand what information the model exploits while performing the task.

To explore these issues, we focus on the SET+POS task and the best-performing FiLM model, and build 7 new training settings with an increasing proportion of *unexpected* cases.[1] Such examples are obtained by simply swapping the original size adjective and its ground-truth answer, as described in Figure 1. By training the model on each of these settings, we show that very little *unexpected* data is needed to obtain high generalizations in testing, and that seeing these examples is beneficial to learn the rule subtending the task.

2 Generalizing to *Unexpected* Data

Method We explore whether injecting some *unexpected* cases in training data helps the model understand the relation that holds between the adjectives 'big' and 'small'. We use the 10K-datapoint (8K training, 1K val, 1K test) SET+POS dataset (hence, A) used by Pezzelle and Fernández (2019) in their *compositional* experiment, and build 7 new training settings containing an increasing percentage of *unexpected* examples. We refer to these settings using capital letters from B to H. They contain 0.8%, 1.6%, 3.2%, 6.4%, 12.8%, 25.6%, and 50.0% *unexpected* cases, respectively. To generate the new training settings, we sample a given percentage of datapoints (e.g., 0.8% for B) from the original training/validation files and simply

swap the original adjective and ground-truth answer (see Figure 1). While doing so, we ensure that a balanced number of cases is modified for each <adjective-noun, ground truth> tuple. To illustrate, out of the 8 modified cases in the validation split of B, 2 involve circles; out of these, one is originally a <big-circle, true> case, the other a <big-circle, false>. This makes all 7 settings perfectly balanced with respect to shape, size, and ground truth.[2] This prevents biases in the data, e.g., that circles are more likely to be *big* than squares. It is worth mentioning that, compared to A, only (some) sentences and answers are modified. As for the visual data, all settings employ the exact same 10K images and visual features precomputed using ResNet-101 (He et al., 2016).

Model We experiment with FiLM (Perez et al., 2018) using the best configuration of hyperparameters and the same experimental pipeline reported in Pezzelle and Fernández (2019). In each setting, the model is trained for 40 epochs with 3 random initializations. For each of these 3 runs, the best model epoch based on accuracy on the validation split is selected and then tested on 3 different test sets: (a) *seen* (1K datapoints), where all the examples are *expected*, (b) *unseen* (1K), where all the examples are *unexpected*, and (c) *balanced* (2K), where a balanced number of *expected* and *unexpected* cases is present. All test sets are taken from Pezzelle and Fernández (2019).

Results In Table 1 we report, for each setting, average model accuracy and standard deviation (sd) over 3 runs (the same results are visualized in Figure 2). Starting from the *unseen* test set, we notice that injecting an extremely low percentage of *unexpected* cases in B (0.8%, i.e., 64/8000 cases in training) has already some impact on the accuracy, with a 12-point increase (27%) compared to A (15%). This pattern is observed in the subsequent settings, with accuracy increasing to 44% in C and to 45% in D. The most striking result is observed in setting E, where model accuracy gets well above chance level (65%) with a percentage of just 6.4% *unexpected* cases seen in training (see also Figure 2, where the blue line exceeds chance level in E). This clearly indicates that the model, instead of just trying to correctly predict all the *expected* cases, which would potentially lead to a

---

[1] Data, code, and trained models are available at: `https://github.com/sandropezzelle/malevic`.

[2] Note that we do not balance with respect to color since this would increase by 5 the number of modified examples.

test set	average accuracy ± sd								
	A [0.0]*	**B [0.8]**	**C [1.6]**	**D [3.2]**	**E [6.4]**	**F [12.8]**	**G [25.6]**	**H [50.0]**	**16K [50.0]***
seen	**0.85 ± 0.01**	0.84 ± 0.02	0.83 ± 0.04	0.74 ± 0.01	0.75 ± 0.04	0.81 ± 0.01	0.74 ± 0.03	0.75 ± 0.01	0.91 ± 0.02
unseen	0.15 ± 0.02	0.27 ± 0.03	0.44 ± 0.00	0.45 ± 0.03	0.65 ± 0.04	0.74 ± 0.03	0.72 ± 0.02	**0.75 ± 0.03**	0.90 ± 0.02
balanced	0.50 ± 0.00	0.54 ± 0.03	0.65 ± 0.04	0.60 ± 0.01	0.71 ± 0.05	**0.79 ± 0.03**	0.73 ± 0.03	0.77 ± 0.03	0.88 ± 0.02

Table 1: Average accuracy ± standard deviation by FiLM on 3 test sets in settings A-H (in brackets, proportion of *unexpected* cases seen in training). For comparison, performance by best model trained with 16K datapoints is reported (16K). * refers to models trained in Pezzelle and Fernández (2019). In **bold**, highest number in the row.

93.6% accuracy, employs a learning strategy that is valuable also for *unexpected* examples.

It is interesting to note, in this regard, that on the *seen* test set the model experiences a performance drop from A (85%) to H (75%), which shows how an increasing proportion of *unexpected* cases makes guessing the *expected* ones a bit harder (this is, to some extent, intuitive since in A there are only 4 *seen* adjective-noun combinations); indeed, the overall best accuracy in *seen* is obtained with A, while the best accuracy in *unseen* is obtained with H, where the highest proportion of *unexpected* examples is given in training. As for the *balanced* test set, we observe that an increasing proportion of *unexpected* cases in training boosts model generalization, though F turns out to slightly outperform H (79% vs 77%) due to its better performance on the *expected* (*seen*) instances. Finally, it should be noted that training with twice as many samples (16K) leads to a significantly higher accuracy in all test sets (+11-16 points compared to H), which shows a 'the bigger, the better' effect of training set size on model performance in the task.

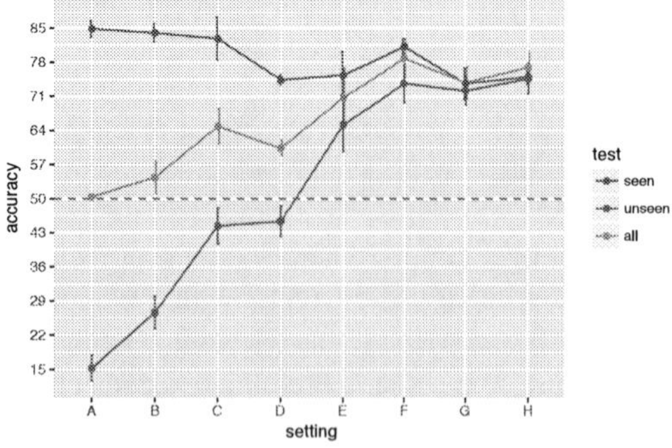

Figure 2: FiLM performance on 3 test sets across settings A-H. Average accuracy over 3 runs (dots) and standard deviation (bars) are reported. The red dashed line indicates chance level. Best viewed in color.

3 Analysis

Linguistic representations In FiLM, the representation of the sentence obtained via the Gated Recurrent Unit (GRU; Chung et al., 2014) influences the CNN computation to focus on image features that are important to solve the task. Thus, examining it could shed light on the type of linguistic information exploited by the model. Here, we are interested in checking how much *size* information is encoded by the GRU in each setting. We run each setting's best trained model on the *balanced* test set and, for each sentence, we extract the final 4096-d GRU hidden state. We then perform a 2-dimensional PCA analysis on these 2K embeddings: if the model pays attention to size adjectives, embeddings containing 'big' ('small') should be overall similar/close to each other, but different/far from those containing 'small' ('big').

In Figure 3, we plot the results of the PCA analysis for settings A, B, C, and H (from left to right). In A, where each shape type is always either 'big' or 'small', embeddings are clearly grouped in 4 clusters corresponding to each shape (labels not reported for clarity of presentation), while no pattern regarding size is observed (i.e., red and blue dots are mixed together). This shows that, in A, the GRU does not learn a specific representation for 'big' and 'small', in line with the hypothesis that the model just ignores these words (Pezzelle and Fernández, 2019). This is confirmed by the results of an additional analysis where we tested the models trained in A on sentences (either from the *seen* or *unseen* test set) from which the size adjective is removed (e.g., 'The white rectangle is a rectangle'). As conjectured, no differences in accuracy compared to the standard setting were observed (i.e., 0.85 in *seen*; 0.15 in *unseen*). In B, in contrast, some information about size is encoded (embeddings containing a 'big' shape are 'South-East' to those containing the same shape 'small'), with this pattern becoming clearer in C, where 'big' and 'small' are neatly separated by

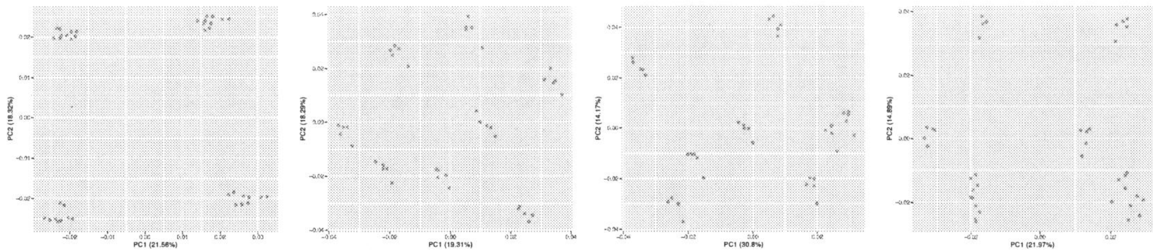

Figure 3: PCA analysis on 2K GRU sentence embeddings by each best model on the *balanced* test set in settings A, B, C, and H (from left to right). Red dots correspond to sentences embedding 'big', blue to 'small'. 'Big', 'small' become progressively separated as the proportion of *unexpected* samples increases. Best viewed in color.

PC1. This distance increases in the subsequent settings (not reported), and becomes extreme in H, where the size adjective is the most discriminative linguistic feature. By testing the models trained in H on the 'without adjective' test sentences, indeed, we obtain an accuracy that is close to chance level (i.e., 0.49 in *seen*; 0.53 in *unseen*), which clearly indicates that the model is unable to perform the task without the size adjective. In sum, seeing more and more *unexpected* cases helps the model develop an increasingly specific, mutually exclusive representation of size adjectives, which goes hand in hand with a better performance.

To quantitatively assess this pattern, we evaluate the similarity between 'big'/'small' embeddings by (1) averaging all the embeddings containing the same adjective, (2) computing the cosine similarity between the two centroids. If the model progressively develops a mutually exclusive representation for 'big' and 'small', the similarity should decrease across settings; in contrast, such a pattern should not be found for shape (the meaning of, e.g., *square* is not supposed to change).[3] The expected pattern is shown in Figure 4, with similarity starting very high in A and rapidly decreasing with an increasing proportion of *unexpected* cases. Note that, in A, there is almost no difference between 'big' and 'small'. This is somehow intuitive since, in the *balanced* test set, the sentences in the 'big' centroid are exactly the same as those in the 'small' one, except for the size adjective. As for shape, a rather 'flat' pattern is observed.

Mutual exclusivity of predictions An insightful way to test whether FiLM has learned a mutually exclusive representation for 'big' and 'small' is to consider its predictions for the orig-

inal (ORIG) and swapped (SWAP) test samples. If the model has learned that being *big* implies being *not small*, and vice versa, we should expect it not to output the same answer (e.g., *true*) to both questions. To explore this issue, we first obtain model predictions on both the *seen* and *unseen* test set. We then take either test set and, for each sample, we swap the size adjective and the ground truth (see Figure 1). This way, we obtain two SWAP test sets where ground truths are systematically reversed compared to ORIG. We obtain model predictions on each SWAP test set, compare them to those on the corresponding ORIG, and count the number of non-overlapping (i.e., mutually exclusive) predictions. As shown in Figure 5, mutual exclusivity is close to 0 in A, where FiLM outputs (almost) always the same answer to both ORIG and SWAP samples, and progressively increases across settings, which boosts FiLM's generalization ability. This pattern of results is in line with what is reported by Gandhi and Lake (2019), i.e., that standard neural networks lack the ability to reason with mutual exclusivity. Until there is a balanced enough number of 'big' and 'small' ex-

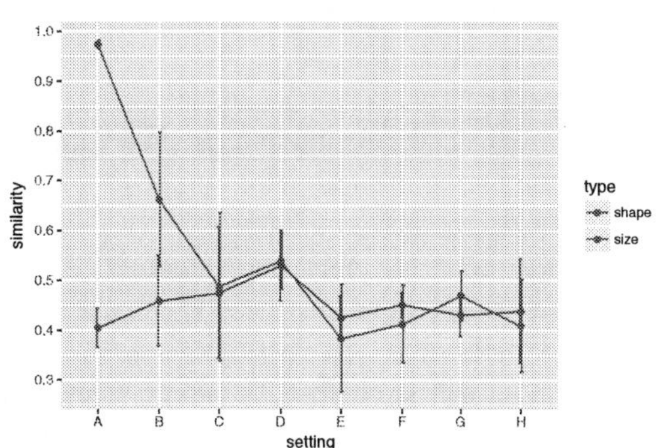

Figure 4: Similarity between sentence embeddings grouped by *shape* or *size*. Best viewed in color.

---

[3]For shape, we obtain an average representation for each shape (*circle*, *square*, etc.), compute all pairwise similarities between the 4 centroids, and compute the average similarity.

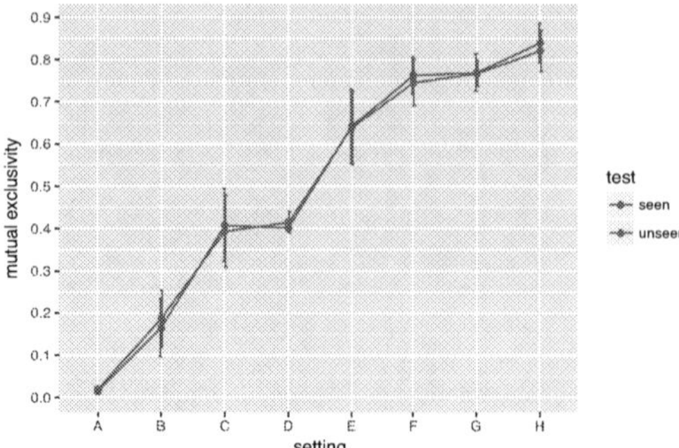

Figure 5: Mutual exclusivity (ME) of predictions between ORIG and SWAP *seen/unseen*. The less overlapping predictions, the higher ME. Best viewed in color.

amples in training, indeed, the model does not fully *understand* the mutually exclusive relation tying the two adjectives; rather, it makes predictions that are biased toward the most frequent, *expected* instances.

4 Generalization vs Compositionality

The results described above show the ability of FiLM to make powerful generalizations with little data. However, this is not informative of its *compositional* skills since, in settings B-H, the same proportion of *unexpected* cases is seen by the model for each shape type. As a consequence, the model is not required to apply the 'big'/'small' relation learned for, say, circles to, say, squares. Here, we test whether learning the rule for some shape types makes the model able to apply it to other shapes. Crucially, this is different from the compositional experiment in Pezzelle and Fernández (2019) (here referred to as setting A) where the 'big'/'small' relation had to be learned across shapes.

We train the model with perfectly balanced data (as in H) for triangles and circles, and perfectly unbalanced data (as in A) for squares and rectangles. More in detail, the model is trained with sentences containing the following queries:[4] *big triangle* (1K datapoints), *small triangle* (1K), *big circle* (1K), *small circle* (1K), *small square* (2K), *big rectangle* (2K), and is then tested with the usual *seen* and *unseen* test sets. If the model learns the abstract, mutually exclusive relation between 'big' and 'small' by being exposed to examples of these two adjectives combined with two different shape

---

[4]We employ the same 8K training datapoints and images used in the previous experiments.

types, it should then be able to *compositionally* apply the rule to the other two types of shape. Otherwise, a similar pattern as the one observed in setting A should be found for squares and rectangles.

On the *seen* test set, where all the adjective-noun combinations are seen in training, the model obtains an average accuracy (over 3 runs) of 0.81. On the *unseen* one, in contrast, it stops at 0.64. As expected, this worse performance is due to the extremely low accuracy on *big square* (0.22) and *small rectangle* (0.23), i.e., the cases that were never seen in training. This opposite pattern of results (triangle and circle vs square and rectangle) suggests that the model learns a 'big'/'small' rule that is shape-dependent and cannot be *compositionally* applied to other shapes. This is confirmed by the results obtained when testing the model on the 'without adjective' test sentences: in the best model run, e.g., chance-level accuracy is observed for triangles and circles in either test set (i.e., the model 'needs' the adjective to perform the task), while the same numbers as those obtained with the default sentences are observed for squares and rectangles (i.e., the adjective is 'ignored').

5 Conclusion

Previous work has reported the inability of FiLM to apply 'big', 'small' to *unseen* adjective-noun combinations (Pezzelle and Fernández, 2019). Here, we show that seeing some of these cases in training mitigates the problem, leading to high generalizations (in line with Lake and Baroni, 2018) and helping the model understand the mutually exclusive status of size adjectives. Although the model can learn the 'big'/'small' rule, this rule is shown to be shape-dependent; i.e., it cannot be learned for some nouns and *compositionally* applied to others for which direct evidence was not observed during training. Taken together, these findings indicate that models fail to apply rules *compositionally*, but are extremely good at generalizing to even rarely *seen* examples.

Acknowledgments

We are grateful to the anonymous reviewers of the LANTERN workshop for their valuable feedback. This work was funded by the Netherlands Organisation for Scientific Research (NWO) under VIDI grant no. 276-89-008, *Asymmetry in Conversation*.

References

Aishwarya Agrawal, Dhruv Batra, Devi Parikh, and Aniruddha Kembhavi. 2018. Don't just assume; look and answer: Overcoming priors for visual question answering. In *Proceedings of the IEEE Conference on Computer Vision and Pattern Recognition*, pages 4971–4980.

Aishwarya Agrawal, Aniruddha Kembhavi, Dhruv Batra, and Devi Parikh. 2017. C-VQA: A compositional split of the Visual Question Answering (VQA) v1.0 dataset. *arXiv preprint arXiv:1704.08243*.

Marco Baroni. 2019. Linguistic generalization and compositionality in modern artificial neural networks. ArXiv preprint arXiv:1904.00157, to appear in the Philosophical Transactions of the Royal Society B.

Junyoung Chung, Caglar Gulcehre, Kyunghyun Cho, and Yoshua Bengio. 2014. Empirical evaluation of gated recurrent neural networks on sequence modeling. In *Workshop on Deep Learning at NIPS-2014*.

Kanishk Gandhi and Brenden M Lake. 2019. Mutual exclusivity as a challenge for neural networks. *arXiv preprint arXiv:1906.10197*.

Kaiming He, Xiangyu Zhang, Shaoqing Ren, and Jian Sun. 2016. Deep residual learning for image recognition. In *Proceedings of the IEEE conference on computer vision and pattern recognition*, pages 770–778.

Justin Johnson, Bharath Hariharan, Laurens van der Maaten, Li Fei-Fei, C Lawrence Zitnick, and Ross Girshick. 2017. CLEVR: A diagnostic dataset for compositional language and elementary visual reasoning. In *Proceedings of the IEEE Conference on Computer Vision and Pattern Recognition*, pages 2901–2910.

Kris Korrel, Dieuwke Hupkes, Verna Dankers, and Elia Bruni. 2019. Transcoding compositionally: Using attention to find more generalizable solutions. In *Proceedings of the 2019 ACL Workshop BlackboxNLP: Analyzing and Interpreting Neural Networks for NLP*, pages 1–11, Florence, Italy. Association for Computational Linguistics.

Brenden Lake and Marco Baroni. 2018. Generalization without systematicity: On the compositional skills of sequence-to-sequence recurrent networks. In *International Conference on Machine Learning*, pages 2879–2888.

Joao Loula, Marco Baroni, and Brenden Lake. 2018. Rearranging the familiar: Testing compositional generalization in recurrent networks. In *Proceedings of the 2018 EMNLP Workshop BlackboxNLP: Analyzing and Interpreting Neural Networks for NLP*, pages 108–114.

Ethan Perez, Florian Strub, Harm De Vries, Vincent Dumoulin, and Aaron Courville. 2018. Film: Visual reasoning with a general conditioning layer. In *Thirty-Second AAAI Conference on Artificial Intelligence*.

Sandro Pezzelle and Raquel Fernández. 2019. Is the Red Square Big? MALeViC: Modeling Adjectives Leveraging Visual Contexts. In *Proceedings of the 2019 Conference on Empirical Methods in Natural Language Processing and 9th International Joint Conference on Natural Language Processing*. Forthcoming.

Sainandan Ramakrishnan, Aishwarya Agrawal, and Stefan Lee. 2018. Overcoming language priors in visual question answering with adversarial regularization. In *Advances in Neural Information Processing Systems*, pages 1541–1551.

Lauren A Schmidt, Noah D Goodman, David Barner, and Joshua B Tenenbaum. 2009. How tall is tall? Compositionality, statistics, and gradable adjectives. In *Proceedings of the 31st annual Conference of the Cognitive Science Society*, pages 2759–2764.

Eigencharacter: An Embedding of Chinese Character Orthography

Yu-Hsiang Tseng
Graduate Institute of Linguistics
National Taiwan Unviersity
seantyh@ntu.edu.tw

Shu-Kai Hsieh
Graduate Institute of Linguistics
National Taiwan Unviersity
shukaihsieh@ntu.edu.tw

Abstract

Chinese characters are unique in its logographic nature, which inherently encodes world knowledge through thousands of years evolution. This paper proposes an embedding approach, namely eigencharacter (EC) space, which helps NLP application easily access the knowledge encoded in Chinese orthography. These EC representations are automatically extracted, encode both structural and radical information, and easily integrate with other computational models. We built EC representations of 5,000 Chinese characters, investigated orthography knowledge encoded in ECs, and demonstrated how these ECs identified visually similar characters with both structural and radical information.

1 Introduction

Chinese is unique in its logographic writing system. The Chinese scripts consists of a sequence of characters, each carried rich linguistic information on its own. Chinese characters are not only mediums for pronunciations and lexical meanings, they also carry abundant information in the visual patterns.

Chinese orthography has been closely investigated in literature, from structural analysis of *ShuoWenJieZi* in Han dynasty, to contemporary sociolinguistic perspective (Tsou, 1981). Recent behavioral studies even argued that, given the salience of Chinese writing system, the orthographic components are activated first when reading, followed by phonological and semantic activation (Perfetti et al., 2005). However, emphases of previous orthographic approaches were more on radicals, components, or their respective positions in the whole characters and how Chinese readers recognize characters in a processing the-

ory. This paper presents a computational approach, eigencharacter representations, to describe Chinese characters in a vector space. The resulting representations encode lexical knowledge embedded in Chinese characters, therefore provide unique insights on the integration between computational models and linguistics.

2 Previous Works

Chinese characters are visual patterns occupied in a square space. Depending on the strokes of a character, the visual pattern may be simple, such as a single stroke character (一, yī, "one") or complex, such as a 16 stroke character (龜, guī, "turtle"). Psychophysics studies showed that Chinese characters carry more information in high spatial frequency, compared with alphabetic language (Wang and Legge, 2018). Although some Chinese characters are *unique* characters, which there is no further components can be distinguished in the whole character, identifying radicals and components in a character is the most common way to analyze Chinese orthography.

2.1 Components decomposition

In Chinese classic text, *ShuoWenJieZi* identified 540 radicals in Chinese characters, from which 214 of them are derived and used in modern Chinese. The radical often carries a semantic meaning of a character, and rest of the characters form a component which may provide hints of character pronunciation. For example, 燃, rán, "burning" has radical 火, huǒ, "fire", in the left side, which has apparent semantic connection between the whole character. The right side of the character, 然, rán, "then" provides a phonological cue, which is the same as the whole character in this exam-

Proceedings of the Beyond Vision and LANguage: inTEgrating Real-world kNowledge (LANTERN), pages 24–28
Hong Kong, China, November 3, 2019. ©2019 Association for Computational Linguistics

ple. The decomposition strategy are especially useful in pedagogical context and behavioral experiment, since it separates meanings from pronunciations, so they can be taught or manipulated separately.

Not all Chinese characters are applicable to this decomposition strategy. Some characters has *unique* structure, which it cannot be easily separated as radical and components. For instance, 東, dōng, "east" has radical of 木, mù, "wood", but the rest of the character, 日, yuē, "say", is tightly embedded in the character and has no phonological relations with the whole character. There are even some characters cannot be decomposed at all, such as 我, wǒ, "I, me", cannot be decomposed into a component after removing the radical (戈, gē, "weaponery").

Some studies tried to decompose characters into finer components, through which characters can be divided recursively into a component hierarchy (Chuang and Hsieh, 2005). For example, instead of decomposing 燃 into its semantic radical (火) and phonological component (然), the phonological component can be further divided into three components: 夕, xì, "dusk", 犬, quǎn, "dog", 灬, huǒ, "fire". This approach provides a complete description of characters, but is not without caveats. Specifically, it is not easy to find visually similar characters with component hierarchy, (e.g. 已 and 己 are visually similar, while not sharing common components), and the definition of a components is not always clear (e.g. 龍, lóng, dragon could have one, two or three components, depending on different definitions).

2.2 Eigendecomposition of Visual Stimuli

Although decomposing characters into components are advantageous in pedagogical context and in behavioral experiments, the discrete nature of components prevents a simple coding scheme of Chinese orthography. Specifically, there are 214 radicals in modern Chinese, which would require hundreds of dimension in a vector to encode radicals and other components. In addition, were positions of each radicals/components considered, the dimensions needed to encoded a single character would increase exponentially.

An alternative approach to construct a computational representation of Chinese character is leveraging the fact scripts are written in square blocks, each character can be considered as an information-laden visual patterns. The computation task is to extract common components among these patterns (characters), and choose fewest possible number of components to best represent given set of characters. The idea is closely related to eigenface decomposition in face recognition and face processing studies (Sirovich and Kirby, 1987).

Chinese characters and faces are two distant but striking similar concepts, both in computational tasks and in cognitive neuroscience. Face and characters were shown to share similar processing mechanisms and even found to have closely related neural mechanisms (Farah et al., 1995; Zhang et al., 2018). In addition, face and (handwritten) character recognition were both attempted in a low dimensional space (Sirovich and Kirby, 1987; Long et al., 2011). The low dimensional face space (eigenface) was later applied into cognitive science, through which a face space was constructed and was used to explain phenomena concerning face recognition (O'toole et al., 1994).

In this paper, inspired by concepts of eigenface, we tried to construct a eigencharacter space to represent Chinese characters, and investigate the orthographic information implicated in eigencharacters.

Constructing eigencharacters provides unique advantages in computational modeling. These representations are invaluable that they are (1) clearly and automatically defined given a set of characters; (2) helpful when finding similar characters even when not sharing common components; (3) insightful when considering Chinese orthography on their structure and essential components; (4) easily manipulable and conveniently incorporated, since they are inherently a vector, into recent computational models (e.g. neural network models).

3 Eigencharacter

We constructed eigencharacter space with 5,000 most frequently used characters, which was the estimated vocabulary size of average college students in Taiwan (Hue, 2003). Mean strokes of these characters was 12.24, standard

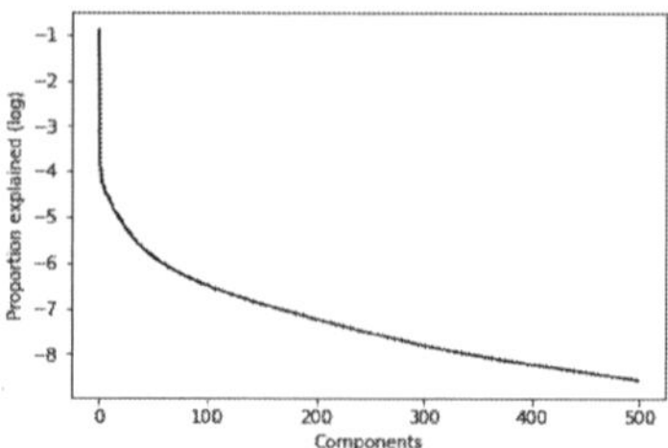

Figure 1: Variance explained under different number of eigencharacter components.

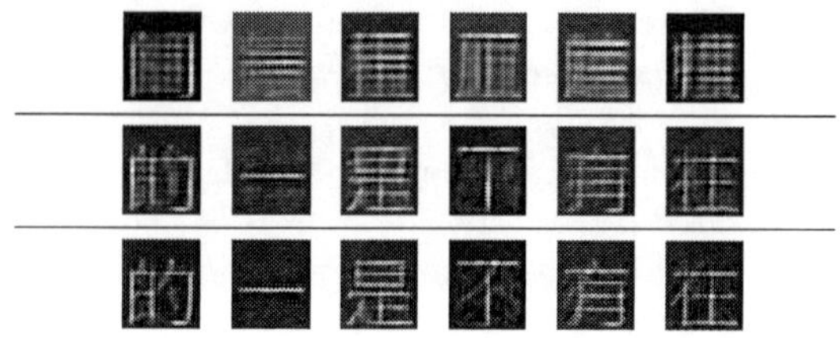

Figure 2: Character reconstructed with different number of eigencharacters. Reconstruction with 10 ECs (upper panel), with 50 ECs (middle panel), and 100 ECs (lower panel).

deviation was 4.48. Character with the fewest stroke (1 stroke) was 一, yī, "one"; the one with most strokes was 籲, yù, "call, implore".

Each character was first drawn with white ink on a binary bitmap of black background. The font used was Microsoft JhenHei, font size was 64. After drawing characters on bitmaps, they were reshaped into column vectors of length 4800 (i.e. 64 × 75). The resulting character matrix therefore has dimension 4800 × 5000 matrix.

The character matrix was then decomposed with singular value decomposition:

$$M = U\Sigma V^T$$

where M is the original character matrix, Σ is a diagonal matrix with singular values. To determine the number of singular vectors, or number of eigencharacters(ECs) needed to best represent the character matrix, we first examined the scree plot of singular values normalized by the Frobenius norm of M (Figure 1).

From Figure 1, proportion of variance explained quickly dropped after 50 ECs. To verified the observation, we attempted to reconstruct the character with first 10, 50 and 100 ECs (i.e. the first 10, 50, 100 columns of U). The resulting construction is shown in Figure 2. The reconstruction of first 10 ECs only recovered limited patterns of each character. Interestingly, the patterns recovered were mostly vertical or horizontal stripes. When using 50 ECs, the resulting patterns started to be recognizable, and they were identifiable when using 100 ECs. Basing on the results above, we chose first 50 ECs to construct eigencharacters space.

4 Experiments

Constructed ECs space serves multiple purposes. Among their potential advantages on incorporating orthographic knowledge naturally inherited in Chinese writing system, we demonstrate how ECs reveal structure and component information in Chinese orthography, and how they are particularly effective in finding visually similar characters.

4.1 Rendering Eigencharacters

ECs are abstract mathematical construct extracted from singular value decomposition, which might not be directly interpretable. However, these ECs are essentially the bases best represent 5,000 characters, the actual patterns of these ECs could bear interesting insight on Chinese orthography.

We rendered 50 ECs extracted in previous section, and reconstructed them as if they were normal character. The renderings were shown in Figure 3, ECs are ordered descendingly by their respective singular values.

The rendering showed interesting patterns. By visual inspection, we can observed that (1) first few ECs encode "low spatial frequency" information, such as the general character block in EC0, vertical stripes in EC1, EC2, and horizontal stripes in EC4, EC5; (2) they do not correspond directly to radicals, but some important radicals can be identified nevertheless, such as 氵 radical, "water" in EC14, 言 radical, "words" in EC15, and 女 radical, "female" in EC31.

In addition to visual inspection, we could also understand ECs by the characters having the highest or the lowest coefficients in each ECs. By these positively or negatively *loaded*

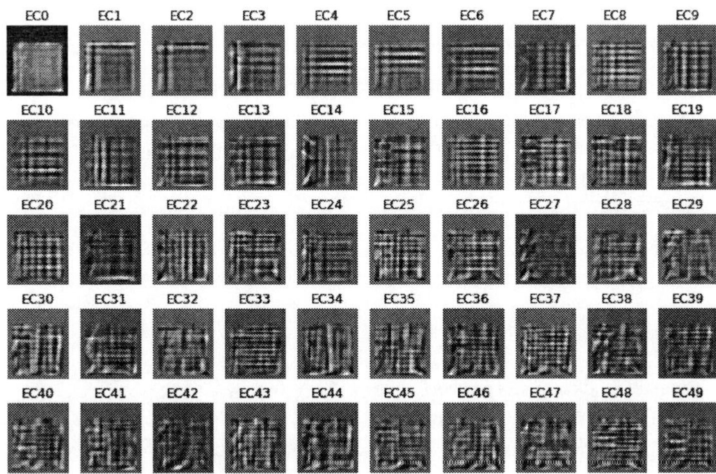

Figure 3: First 50 Eigencharacters.

characters, we could infer the information each EC encodes in character space. For example, the 3 highest loaded characters on EC0 are 轟, 寶 and 鷹, and the 3 lowest loaded characters are 一, 卜, and 二, aided by the EC rendering, we could infer EC0 is a component of "stroke complexity". Likewise, the 3 highest loaded characters of EC1 are 圃, 闔, and 閘, the 3 lowest loaded are 值, 椿, and 捧. EC1 is then infered to be a component of "enclosing structure". These components of structure echoed the behavioral studies that showed Chinese readers use structural information to judge character similarity (Yeh and Li, 2002). Aside from components of structural representation, there are also components of radicals. For instance, EC31, which shows a 女 radical in rendering, is a component of 女 radical. It has highest loading in characters with 女 radical, such as 媒, 娩, and 妮.

Renderings of ECs and inspection of their loaded characters, suggest ECs are not only abstract mathematical constructs. Instead, they automatically encode and reflect structural and radical aspects in Chinese orthography.

4.2 Finding Similar Characters

Eigencharacters encodes structural and radical information in characters, which would be ideal to find visual similar characters that is otherwise impossible using components decomposition approach.

Table 1 show examples of similar characters identified with eigencharacters. Character similarity is defined as the euclidean distance between two characters in EC space. In first row of table 1, EC space found similar characters with identical radical (氵), components(胡), and remarkably considering the three parts vertical structure simultaneously. In the second row of the table, the similar characters of 語, highlighted another property of EC space: it did not restrict itself on the exact components, but the visually similar components, such as 諮, 晤 and 誤, they either share the same radical/component, or having similar right hand side components. The last row also showed the advantages of EC space in finding visually similar character. For instance, 東 and 泉 are both unique structure, and they share similar patterns (日 in the middle, and two oblique strokes in lower half) which would be challenged to accommodate were components-based decomposition were used.

These illustrative examples showed EC space, which inherently equipped with knowledge of structural and radical information, provides an ideal representation to explore Chinese orthography.

5 Conclusion

This paper introduces eigencharacters, an embedding representation of Chinese orthography. It provides unique advantages over

Seed	Similar characters
湖	溯潮漏瑚潤
語	諙唔誤診譜
頭	頬頷頸頌頻
龍	鶴廳籠麓龖
東	泉帛柬車蒐

Table 1: Similar characters found with eigencharacter space.

component-based character decomposition, in that it can be automatically extracted, encodes both structural and radical information, and easily integrates with other computational models. Equipped with EC representations, human knowledge encoded in Chinese orthography becomes easily accessible to downstream NLP applications.

Acknowledgments

This work was supported by Ministry of Science and Technology (MOST), Taiawan. Grant Number MOST 108-2634-F-001-006.

References

D. M. Chuang and C. C. Hsieh. 2005. Database of chinese character orthography: Development and application. In *International conference on Chinese character and globalization*.

Martha J. Farah, Kevin D. Wilson, H. Maxwell Drain, and James R. Tanaka. 1995. The inverted face inversion effect in prosopagnosia: Evidence for mandatory, face-specific perceptual mechanisms. *Vision Research*, 35(14):2089–2093.

C. W. Hue. 2003. Number of characters a college student knows. *Journal of Chinese Linguistics*, 31(2):300–339.

H. Long, X. C. Zhang, and K. E. Ercan. 2011. Handwritten chinese character recognition using eigen space decomposition. *Science China*, 53(1):1–10.

Alice J. O'toole, Kenneth A. Deffenbacher, Dominique Valentin, and Herve Abdi. 1994. Structural aspects of face recognition and the other-race effect. *Memory & Cognition*, 22(2):208–224.

Charles A. Perfetti, Ying Liu, and Li Hai Tan. 2005. The lexical constituency model: Some implications of research on chinese for general theories of reading. *Psychological Review*, 112(1):43–59.

L. Sirovich and M. Kirby. 1987. Low-dimensional procedure for the characterization of human faces. *J. Opt. Soc. Am. A*, 4(3):519–524.

B. K. Y. Tsou. 1981. A sociolinguistic analysis of the logographic writing system of chinese. *Journal of Chinese Linguistics*, 9(1):1–19.

Hui Wang and Gordon E. Legge. 2018. Comparing the minimum spatial-frequency content for recognizing Chinese and alphabet charactersWang amp; Legge. *Journal of Vision*, 18(1):1–1.

Su-Ling Yeh and Jing-Ling Li. 2002. Role of structure and component in judgments of visual similarity of chinese characters. *Journal of Experimental Psychology: Human Perception and Performance*, 28(4):933–947.

Bo Zhang, Sheng He, and Xuchu Weng. 2018. Localization and functional characterization of an occipital visual word form sensitive area. *Scientific Reports*, 8(1).

On the Role of Scene Graphs in Image Captioning

Dalin Wang   **Daniel Beck**   **Trevor Cohn**
School of Computing and Information Systems
The University of Melbourne
`dalinw@student.unimelb.edu.au`
`{d.beck,t.cohn}@unimelb.edu.au`

Abstract

Scene graphs represent semantic information in images, which can help image captioning system to produce more descriptive outputs versus using only the image as context. Recent captioning approaches rely on ad-hoc approaches to obtain graphs for images. However, those graphs introduce noise and it is unclear the effect of parser errors on captioning accuracy. In this work, we investigate to what extent scene graphs can help image captioning. Our results show that a state-of-the-art scene graph parser can boost performance almost as much as the ground truth graphs, showing that the bottleneck currently resides more on the captioning models than on the performance of the scene graph parser.

1 Introduction

The task of automatically recognizing and describing visual scenes in the real world, normally referred to as image captioning, is a long standing problem in computer vision and computational linguistics. Previously proposed methods based on deep neural networks have demonstrated convincing results in this task, (Xu et al., 2015; Lu et al., 2018; Anderson et al., 2018; Lu et al., 2017; Fu et al., 2017; Ren et al., 2017) yet they often produce dry and simplistic captions, which lack descriptive depth and omit key relations between objects in the scene. Incorporating complex visual relations knowledge between objects in the form of scene graphs has the potential to improve captioning systems beyond current limitations.

Scene graphs, such as the ones present in the Visual Genome dataset (Krishna et al., 2017), can be used to incorporate external knowledge into images. Because of the structured abstraction and greater semantic representation capacity than purely image features, they have the potential to improve image captioning, as well as other downstream tasks that rely on visual components. This has led to the development of many parsing algorithms for scene graphs (Li et al., 2018, 2017; Xu et al., 2017; Dai et al., 2017; Yu et al., 2017). Simultaneously, recent work also aimed at incorporating scene graphs into captioning systems, with promising results (Yao et al., 2018; Xu et al., 2019). However, these previous work still rely on ad-hoc scene graph parsers, raising the question of how captioning systems behave under potential parsing errors.

In this work, we aim at answering the following question: "to what degree scene graphs contribute to the performance of image captioning systems?". In order to answer this question we provide two contributions: 1) we investigate the performance of incorporating scene graphs generated by a state-of-the-art scene graph parser (Li et al., 2018) into a well-established image captioning framework (Anderson et al., 2018); and 2) we provide an upper bound on the performance by comparative experiments with *ground truth* graphs. Our results show that scene graphs can be used to boost performance of image captioning, and scene graphs generated by state-of-art scene graph parser, though still limited in the number of objects and relations categories, is not far below the ground-truth graphs, in terms of standard image captioning metrics.

2 Methods

Our architecture, inspired by Anderson et al. (2018) and shown in Figure 1, assumes an off-the-shelf scene graph parser. To improve performance, we also incorporate information from the original image through a set of region features obtained through an object detection model. Note we experiment with each set of features in isolation in

Proceedings of the Beyond Vision and LANguage: inTEgrating Real-world kNowledge (LANTERN), pages 29–34
Hong Kong, China, November 3, 2019. ©2019 Association for Computational Linguistics

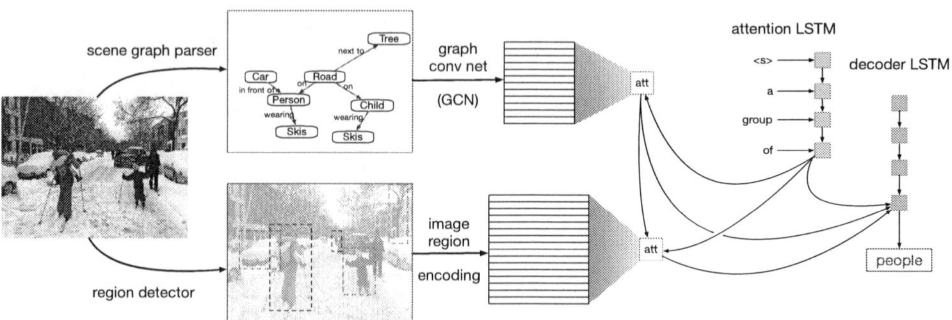

Figure 1: Overview of our architecture for image captioning.

Section 3.1. Given those inputs, our model consists a scene graph encoder, an LSTM-based attention module and another LSTM as the decoder.

2.1 Scene Graph Encoder

The scene graph is represented as a set of *node* embeddings which are then updated into contextual hidden vectors using a Graph Convolutional Network (Kipf and Welling, 2017, GCN). In particular, we employ the GCN version proposed by Marcheggiani and Titov (2017), who incorporate directions and edge labels. We treat each relation and object in the scene graph as nodes, which are then connected with five different types of edges.[1] Since we assume scene graphs are obtained by a parser, they may contain noise in the form of faulty or nugatory connections. To mitigate the influence of parsing errors, we allow edge-wise gating so the network learns to prune those connections. We refer to Marcheggiani and Titov (2017) for details of their GCN architecture.

2.2 Attention LSTM

The Attention LSTM keeps track of contextual information from the inputs and incorporates information from the decoder. At each time step t, the Attention LSTM takes in contextual information by concatenating the previous hidden state of the Decoder LSTM, the mean-pooled region-level image features, the mean-pooled scene graph node features from the GCN and the previous generated word representation: $\mathbf{x}_t^1 = [\mathbf{h}_{t-1}^2, \overline{\mathbf{v}}, \overline{\mathbf{f}}, W_e\mathbf{u}_t]$ where W_e is the word embedding matrix for vocabulary Σ and $\mathbf{u}_t$ is the one-hot encoding of the word at time step t. Given the hidden state of the

Attention LSTM h_t^1, we generate cascaded attention features, first over scene graph features, and then we concatenate the attention weighted scene graph features with the hidden state of the Attention LSTM to attend over region-level image features. Here, we only show the second attention step over region-level image features as they are identical procedures except for the input:

$$b_{i,t} = \mathbf{w}_b^T \text{ReLU}(W_{fb}\mathbf{v}_i + W_{hb}[\mathbf{h}_t^1, \hat{\mathbf{f}}_t])$$

$$\beta_t = \text{softmax}(\mathbf{b}_t); \quad \hat{\mathbf{v}}_t = \sum_{i=1}^{N_v} \beta_{i,t}\mathbf{v}_i$$

where $\mathbf{w}_b^T \in \mathbb{R}^H, W_{fb} \in \mathbb{R}^{H \times D_f}, W_{hb} \in \mathbb{R}^{H \times H}$ are learnable weights. $\hat{\mathbf{v}}_t$ and $\hat{\mathbf{f}}_t$ are the attention weighted image features and scene graph features respectively.

2.3 Decoder LSTM

The inputs to the Decoder LSTM consist of the previous hidden state from the Attention LSTM layer, attention weighted scene graph node features, and attention weighted image features. $x_t^2 = [\mathbf{h}_t^1, \hat{\mathbf{f}}_t, \hat{\mathbf{v}}_t]$ Using the notation $y_{1:T}$ to refer to a sequence of words $(y_1, ..., y_T)$ at each time step t, the conditional distribution over possible output words is given by: $p(y_t|y_{1:t-1}) = \text{softmax}(W_p\mathbf{h}_t^2 + \mathbf{b}_p)$ where $W_p \in \mathbb{R}^{|\Sigma| \times H}$ and $\mathbf{b}_p \in \mathbb{R}^{|\Sigma|}$ are learned weights and biases.

2.4 Training and Inference

Given a target ground truth sequence $y_{1:T}^*$ and a captioning model with parameters θ, we minimize the standard cross entropy loss. At inference time, we use beam search with a beam size of 5 and apply length normalization (Wu et al., 2016).

---

[1] We use the following types: *subj* indicates the edge between a subject and predicate, *obj* denotes the edge between a predicate and an object, *subj'* and *obj'*, their corresponding reverse edges, and lastly, *self*, which denotes a self loop.

3   Experiments

Datasets   **MS-COCO**, (Lin et al., 2014) is the most popular benchmark for image captioning, which contains 82,783 training images and 40,504 validation images, with five human-annotated descriptions per image. As the annotations of the official testing set are not publicly available, we follow the widely used Kaparthy split (Karpathy and Fei-Fei, 2017), and take 113,287 images for training, 5K for validation, and 5K for testing. We convert all the descriptions in training set to lower case and discard rare words which occur less than five times, resulting in a vocabulary with 10,201 unique words. For the oracle experiments, we take a subset of MS-COCO that intersects with Visual Genome (Krishna et al., 2017) to obtain the ground truth scene graphs. The resulting dataset (henceforth, *MS-COCO-GT*) contains 33,569 training, 2,108s validation, and 2,116 test images respectively.

Preprocessing   The scene graphs are obtained by a state-of-the-art parser: a pre-trained Factorizable-Net trained on MSDN split (Li et al., 2017), which is a cleaner version of the Visual Genome[2] that consists of 150 object categories and 50 relationship categories. Notice that the number of object categories and relationships are much smaller than the actual number of objects and relationships in the Visual Genome dataset. All the predicted objects are associated with a set of bound box coordinates. The region-level image features[3] are obtained from Faster-RCNN (Ren et al., 2017), which is also trained on Visual Genome, using 1,600 object classes and 400 attributes classes.

Implementation   Our models are trained with AdamMax optimizer (Kingma and Ba, 2015). We set the initial learning rate as 0.001 with a mini-batch size as 256. We set the maximum number of epochs to be 100 with early stopping mechanism.[4] During inference, we set the beam width to 5. Each word in the sentence is represented as a one-hot vector, and each word embedding is a 1,024-

---

	B	M	R	C	S
No edge-wise gating					
I	34.1	26.5	55.5	108.0	19.9
G	22.8	20.6	46.7	66.3	13.5
I+G	34.2	26.5	55.7	108.2	20.1
With edge-wise gating					
G	22.9	21.1	47.5	70.7	14.0
I+G	**34.5**	**26.8**	**55.9**	**108.6**	**20.3**

Table 1: Results on the full MS-COCO dataset. "I", "G" and "I+G" correspond to models using image features only, scene graphs only and both, respectively. "B", "M", "R", "C" and "S" correspond to BLEU, METEOR, ROUGE, CIDEr and SPICE (higher is better).

dimensional vector. For each image, we have $K = 36$ region features with bounding box coordinates from Faster-RCNN. Each region-level image feature is represented as a 2,048-dimensional vector, and we concatenate the bounding box coordinates to each of the region-level image features. The dimension of the hidden layer in each LSTM and GCN layer is set to 1,024. We use two GCN layers in all our experiments.

Evaluation   We employ standard automatic evaluation metrics including BLEU (Papineni et al., 2002), METEOR (Lavie and Agarwal, 2007), ROUGE (Lin, 2004), CIDEr (Vedantam et al., 2015) and SPICE (Anderson et al., 2016), and we use the coco-caption tool[5] to obtain the scores.

3.1   Quantitative Results and Analysis

Table 1 shows the performances of our models against baseline models whose architecture is based on Bottom-up Top-down Attention model (Anderson et al., 2018). Overall, our proposed model incorporating scene graph features achieves better results across all evaluation metrics, compared to image features only or graph features only. The results show that our model can learn to exploit the relational information in scene graphs and effectively integrate those with image features. Moreover, the results also demonstrate the effectiveness of edge-wise gating in pruning noisy scene graph features.

We also conduct experiments comparing Factorizable-Net generated scene graph with ground-truth scene graph, as shown in Table 2. As expected, the results show that the performance is

---

[2]The MSDN split might contain training instances that overlap with the Karpathy split

[3]These regions are different to those from the scene graph. To help the model learn to match regions, the inputs to attention include bounding box coordinates.

[4]We stop training if the CIDEr score does not improve for 10 epochs, and we reduce the learning by 20 percent if the CIDEr score does not improve for 5 epochs.

[5]https://github.com/tylin/coco-caption

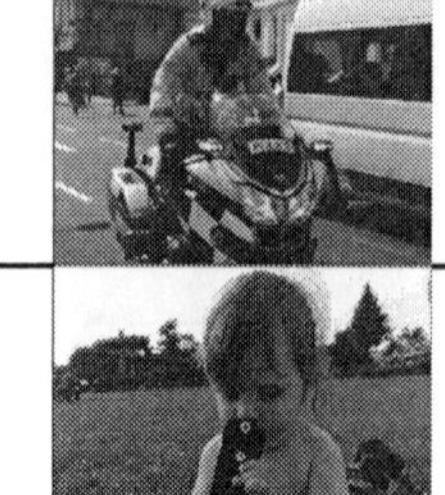

Figure 2: Caption generation results on COCO dataset. All results are generated by models trained on the full version of Karpathy split, and all graph features are processed by GCN with edge-wise gating. 1) Ground Truth(GT) 2) Image features only(Image) 3) Graph features only(Graph) 4) Ours: Image features plus graph features (I + G)

	B	M	R	C	S
I	32.0	25.6	54.3	102.2	19.0
G (pred)	17.4	16.5	41.3	49.5	10.6
G (truth)	18.4	17.9	42.5	50.8	11.2
I+G (pred)	32.2	25.8	54.4	103.4	19.1
I+G (truth)	**32.5**	**26.1**	**54.8**	**105.2**	**19.5**

Table 2: Results on the MS-COCO-GT dataset. "G (pred)" refers to the parsed scene graphs from Factorizable-Net while "G (truth)" corresponds to the ground truth graphs obtained from Visual Genome.

better with ground-truth scene graph. Notably the SPICE score, which measures the semantic correlation between generated captions and ground truth captions, improved by 2.1%, since there are considerably more types of objects, relations and attributes present in the ground-truth scene graphs. Overall, the results show the potential of incorporating automatically generated scene graph features for the captioning system, and we argue with better scene graph parser trained on more objects, relations and attributes categories, the captioning system should provide additional improvements.

Compared to a recent image captioning paper[6] (Li and Jiang, 2019) using scene-graph features, our results are superior, demonstrating the effectiveness of our model. Moreover, compared to a state-of-art image captioning system (Yu et al., 2019),[7] our scores are inferior, as we do not apply scheduled sampling, reinforcement learning,

transformer cell or ensemble predictions, which have all been proven to improve the scores significantly. However, our method of incorporating scene-graph features is orthogonal to the state-of-art methods.

3.2 Qualitative Results and Analysis

Figure 2 shows some generated captions by different approaches trained on the full Karpathy split of MS-COCO dataset. We can see that all approaches can produce sensible captions describing the image content. However, our approach of incorporating scene graph features and image features can generate more descriptive captions that more closely narrate the underlying relations in the image. In the first example, our model correctly predicts that the motercycle is in front of the white van while the image-only model misses this relational detail. On the other hand, purely graph features sometimes introduce noise. As shown in the second example, the graph-only model mistakes the little girl in a park as a woman on a bench, whereas the image features in our model helps disambiguate faulty graph features.

4 Conclusion

We have presented a novel image captioning framework that incorporates scene graph features extracted from state-of-art scene graph parser Factorizable-Net. Particularly, we investigate the problem of integrating relation-aware scene graph features encoded by Graph Convolution with region-level image features to boost image captioning performance. Extensive experiments conducted on MSCOCO image captioning dataset has shown the effectiveness of our method. In the future, we want to experiment with building an

---

[6] The Hierarchical Attention Model incorporating scene-graph features reports scores: Bleu4 33.8, METEOR 26.2, ROUGE 54.9, CIDEr 110.3, SPICE 19.8

[7] This transformer-based captioning system reports scores: Bleu4 40.4, METEOR 29.4, ROUGE 59.6, CIDEr 130.0.

end-to-end multi-task framework that jointly predicts visual relations and captions.

References

Peter Anderson, Basura Fernando, Mark Johnson, and Stephen Gould. 2016. SPICE: semantic propositional image caption evaluation. In *Computer Vision - ECCV 2016 - 14th European Conference, Amsterdam, The Netherlands, October 11-14, 2016, Proceedings, Part V*, pages 382–398.

Peter Anderson, Xiaodong He, Chris Buehler, Damien Teney, Mark Johnson, Stephen Gould, and Lei Zhang. 2018. Bottom-up and top-down attention for image captioning and visual question answering. In *2018 IEEE Conference on Computer Vision and Pattern Recognition, CVPR 2018, Salt Lake City, UT, USA, June 18-22, 2018*, pages 6077–6086.

Bo Dai, Yuqi Zhang, and Dahua Lin. 2017. Detecting visual relationships with deep relational networks. In *2017 IEEE Conference on Computer Vision and Pattern Recognition, CVPR 2017, Honolulu, HI, USA, July 21-26, 2017*, pages 3298–3308.

Kun Fu, Junqi Jin, Runpeng Cui, Fei Sha, and Changshui Zhang. 2017. Aligning where to see and what to tell: Image captioning with region-based attention and scene-specific contexts. *IEEE Trans. Pattern Anal. Mach. Intell.*, 39(12):2321–2334.

Andrej Karpathy and Li Fei-Fei. 2017. Deep visual-semantic alignments for generating image descriptions. *IEEE Trans. Pattern Anal. Mach. Intell.*, 39(4):664–676.

Diederik P. Kingma and Jimmy Ba. 2015. Adam: A method for stochastic optimization. In *3rd International Conference on Learning Representations, ICLR 2015, San Diego, CA, USA, May 7-9, 2015, Conference Track Proceedings*.

Thomas N. Kipf and Max Welling. 2017. Semi-supervised classification with graph convolutional networks. In *5th International Conference on Learning Representations, ICLR 2017, Toulon, France, April 24-26, 2017, Conference Track Proceedings*.

Ranjay Krishna, Yuke Zhu, Oliver Groth, Justin Johnson, Kenji Hata, Joshua Kravitz, Stephanie Chen, Yannis Kalantidis, Li-Jia Li, David A. Shamma, Michael S. Bernstein, and Li Fei-Fei. 2017. Visual genome: Connecting language and vision using crowdsourced dense image annotations. *International Journal of Computer Vision*, 123(1):32–73.

Alon Lavie and Abhaya Agarwal. 2007. METEOR: an automatic metric for MT evaluation with high levels of correlation with human judgments. In *Proceedings of the Second Workshop on Statistical Machine Translation, WMT@ACL 2007, Prague, Czech Republic, June 23, 2007*, pages 228–231.

Xiangyang Li and Shuqiang Jiang. 2019. Know more say less: Image captioning based on scene graphs. *IEEE Trans. Multimedia*, 21(8):2117–2130.

Yikang Li, Wanli Ouyang, Bolei Zhou, Jianping Shi, Chao Zhang, and Xiaogang Wang. 2018. Factorizable net: An efficient subgraph-based framework for scene graph generation. In *Computer Vision - ECCV 2018 - 15th European Conference, Munich, Germany, September 8-14, 2018, Proceedings, Part I*, pages 346–363.

Yikang Li, Wanli Ouyang, Bolei Zhou, Kun Wang, and Xiaogang Wang. 2017. Scene graph generation from objects, phrases and region captions. In *IEEE International Conference on Computer Vision, ICCV 2017, Venice, Italy, October 22-29, 2017*, pages 1270–1279.

Chin-Yew Lin. 2004. ROUGE: A package for automatic evaluation of summaries. In *Text Summarization Branches Out*, pages 74–81, Barcelona, Spain. Association for Computational Linguistics.

Tsung-Yi Lin, Michael Maire, Serge J. Belongie, James Hays, Pietro Perona, Deva Ramanan, Piotr Dollár, and C. Lawrence Zitnick. 2014. Microsoft COCO: common objects in context. In *Computer Vision - ECCV 2014 - 13th European Conference, Zurich, Switzerland, September 6-12, 2014, Proceedings, Part V*, pages 740–755.

Jiasen Lu, Caiming Xiong, Devi Parikh, and Richard Socher. 2017. Knowing when to look: Adaptive attention via a visual sentinel for image captioning. In *2017 IEEE Conference on Computer Vision and Pattern Recognition, CVPR 2017, Honolulu, HI, USA, July 21-26, 2017*, pages 3242–3250.

Jiasen Lu, Jianwei Yang, Dhruv Batra, and Devi Parikh. 2018. Neural baby talk. In *2018 IEEE Conference on Computer Vision and Pattern Recognition, CVPR 2018, Salt Lake City, UT, USA, June 18-22, 2018*, pages 7219–7228.

Diego Marcheggiani and Ivan Titov. 2017. Encoding sentences with graph convolutional networks for semantic role labeling. In *Proceedings of the 2017 Conference on Empirical Methods in Natural Language Processing, EMNLP 2017, Copenhagen, Denmark, September 9-11, 2017*, pages 1506–1515.

Kishore Papineni, Salim Roukos, Todd Ward, and Wei-Jing Zhu. 2002. Bleu: a method for automatic evaluation of machine translation. In *Proceedings of the 40th Annual Meeting of the Association for Computational Linguistics, July 6-12, 2002, Philadelphia, PA, USA.*, pages 311–318.

Shaoqing Ren, Kaiming He, Ross B. Girshick, and Jian Sun. 2017. Faster R-CNN: towards real-time object detection with region proposal networks. *IEEE Trans. Pattern Anal. Mach. Intell.*, 39(6):1137–1149.

Ramakrishna Vedantam, C. Lawrence Zitnick, and Devi Parikh. 2015. Cider: Consensus-based image description evaluation. In *IEEE Conference on Computer Vision and Pattern Recognition, CVPR 2015, Boston, MA, USA, June 7-12, 2015*, pages 4566–4575.

Yonghui Wu, Mike Schuster, Zhifeng Chen, Quoc V. Le, Mohammad Norouzi, Wolfgang Macherey, Maxim Krikun, Yuan Cao, Qin Gao, Klaus Macherey, Jeff Klingner, Apurva Shah, Melvin Johnson, Xiaobing Liu, ukasz Kaiser, Stephan Gouws, Yoshikiyo Kato, Taku Kudo, Hideto Kazawa, and Jeffrey Dean. 2016. Google's neural machine translation system: Bridging the gap between human and machine translation.

Danfei Xu, Yuke Zhu, Christopher B. Choy, and Li Fei-Fei. 2017. Scene graph generation by iterative message passing. In *2017 IEEE Conference on Computer Vision and Pattern Recognition, CVPR 2017, Honolulu, HI, USA, July 21-26, 2017*, pages 3097–3106.

Kelvin Xu, Jimmy Ba, Ryan Kiros, Kyunghyun Cho, Aaron C. Courville, Ruslan Salakhutdinov, Richard S. Zemel, and Yoshua Bengio. 2015. Show, attend and tell: Neural image caption generation with visual attention. In *Proceedings of the 32nd International Conference on Machine Learning, ICML 2015, Lille, France, 6-11 July 2015*, pages 2048–2057.

Ning Xu, An-An Liu, Jing Liu, Weizhi Nie, and Yuting Su. 2019. Scene graph captioner: Image captioning based on structural visual representation. *J. Visual Communication and Image Representation*, 58:477–485.

Ting Yao, Yingwei Pan, Yehao Li, and Tao Mei. 2018. Exploring visual relationship for image captioning. In *Computer Vision - ECCV 2018 - 15th European Conference, Munich, Germany, September 8-14, 2018, Proceedings, Part XIV*, pages 711–727.

Jun Yu, Jing Li, Zhou Yu, and Qingming Huang. 2019. Multimodal transformer with multi-view visual representation for image captioning. *CoRR*, abs/1905.07841.

Ruichi Yu, Ang Li, Vlad I. Morariu, and Larry S. Davis. 2017. Visual relationship detection with internal and external linguistic knowledge distillation. In *IEEE International Conference on Computer Vision, ICCV 2017, Venice, Italy, October 22-29, 2017*, pages 1068–1076.

Understanding the Effect of Textual Adversaries in Multimodal Machine Translation

Koel Dutta Chowdhury
Dept. of Language Science and Technology
Saarland University, Germany
`koeldc@lst.uni-saarland.de`

Desmond Elliott
Department of Computer Science
University of Copenhagen
`de@di.ku.dk`

Abstract

It is assumed that multimodal machine translation systems are better than text-only systems at translating phrases that have a direct correspondence in the image. This assumption has been challenged in experiments demonstrating that state-of-the-art multimodal systems perform equally well in the presence of randomly selected images, but, more recently, it has been shown that masking entities from the source language sentence during training can help to overcome this problem. In this paper, we conduct experiments with both visual and textual adversaries in order to understand the role of incorrect textual inputs to such systems. Our results show that when the source language sentence contains mistakes, multimodal translation systems do not leverage the additional visual signal to produce the correct translation. We also find that the degradation of translation performance caused by textual adversaries is significantly higher than by visual adversaries.

1 Introduction

There has been a surge of interest in tackling machine translation problems using additional information, such as a image or video context. It has been claimed that systems trained on a combination of visual and textual inputs produce better translations than systems trained using only textual inputs (Specia et al., 2016; Elliott et al., 2017). However, these claims have been the subject of debate in the literature: Elliott (2018) argued that the additional visual input is not necessarily used by demonstrating that the performance of a system did not change when it was evaluated with randomly selected images, and Grönroos et al. (2018) observed that their models were insensitive to being evaluated with an "averaged" visual vector, as opposed to the expected visual vector. More recently, Caglayan et al. (2019) presented experiments in which the colour and entity tokens (e.g.

blue or *woman*) were masked during the training of a multimodal translation model. They found that training the model under these conditions resulted in the system relying on the visual modality to recover the masked words during evaluation. Although, their results show that the visual modality can be used to recover the masked tokens in the source sentences, it is not clear if these systems will perform similarly when there is a *mismatch* between the textual and visual concepts.

In this paper, we explore the effect of textual adversaries in multimodal machine translation. We construct hard negative textual adversaries, which contradict the original meaning, in order to explore the robustness of systems to textual adversaries. The textual adversaries are based on minimal manipulations to the sentences, for example:

(1)   a.   Two people walking on the beach.
       b.   *Two people walking on the grass.

The adversarial sentence (1b) still retains most aspects of the original sentence but it depicts a completely unrelated scene. In our experiments, we study how significantly these types of textual perturbations affect the performance of multimodal translation systems. If a system is sufficiently modelling the visual modality, we expect it to ignore this type of perturbation, and to produce the correct translation by leveraging the visual input.

The main contribution of this paper is an evaluation of multimodal translation systems in the presence of adversarial textual data. This evaluation is based on four types of textual adversaries described in Section 2. We evaluate the effect of these adversaries on three state-of-the-art systems, and we also probe the visual awareness of these models by exposing them to randomly selected images. Our results show that although these systems are not greatly affected by the visual adver-

Proceedings of the Beyond Vision and LANguage: inTEgrating Real-world kNowledge (LANTERN), pages 35–40
Hong Kong, China, November 3, 2019. ©2019 Association for Computational Linguistics

Type	Original	Adversarial
Num	<u>Two</u> people walking on the beach.	*Four* people walking on the beach.
Noun	Two people walking on the <u>beach</u>.	Two people walking on the *grass*.
NP	<u>Two people</u> walking on <u>the beach</u>.	*The beach* walking on *two people*.
Prep	Two people walking <u>on</u> the beach.	Two people walking *through* the beach.

Figure 1: Examples of adversarial textual samples that we use to attack the multimodal translation models. The underlined text denotes the words or phrases that are perturbed to create the adversarial example.

saries, they are substantially affected by the textual adversaries.

2 Generating Textual Adversaries

We define *visual term* as a word or phrase that can be expected to be clearly illustrated in an image. In our experiments, we evaluate the performance of multimodal translation systems by modifying a *visual term* in a sentence to create a textual adversary. We create four types of adversarial samples following the methodology introduced in Young et al. (2014); Hodosh and Hockenmaier (2016); Shi et al. (2018) [1] The adversaries are constructed from syntactic analyses of the sentences using POS tagging, chunking, and dependency parses from the SpaCy toolkit (Honnibal and Johnson, 2015). Figure 1 presents an overview and examples of each type of adversary.

Replace Numeral (Num): Our simplest adversary is to replace the numeral in a sentence with a different quantity. We detect the tokens in a sentence that represent numbers (based on their part-of-speech tags) and replace them with alternative numerals. In addition, we treat the indefinite articles "a" and "an" as the numeral "one" because they are typically used as numerals in image captions. Furthermore, subsequent noun phrase chunks are either singularized or pluralized accordingly. We expect that this will have a small effect on translation quality unless the adversary introduces a serious inconsistency with the image.

Replace Noun Head (Noun): We extract the list of all concrete noun heads (Zwicky, 1985) from the COCO dataset (Chen et al., 2015) and swap them with the noun heads in our data. We compute concreteness[2] following Turney et al. (2011) and only consider words with concreteness

measure $\theta > 0.6$. We use WordNet (Miller, 1998) heuristic hypernymy rules to replace noun heads with terms that are semantically different.

(2)   a.   The girl plays with the LEGOs.
         b.   The girl plays with the bricks.
         c.   *The girl plays with the giraffes.

If our aim is to create an adversarial sentence, given 2(a), then 2(b) is too semantically similar and does not create a good adversarial example. However, (2c) creates a better adversarial example because "giraffes" are more semantically different to "LEGOs" than "bricks". We hypothesize that the system should heavily rely on the information contained in the visual model and discard these errors to produce correct translation.

Switch Noun Phrases (NP): For each sentence, the position of the extracted noun phrases are switched. In the example in Figure 1, we refer to *two people* and *the beach* respectively as the partitive first noun phrase (NP_1) and second noun phrase (NP_2). The position of NP_1 and NP_2 are switched. As a result, the new sentence depicts a different scene. Such examples allow us to evaluate whether the models can identify important changes in word-order.

Replace Preposition (Prep): Finally, we detect the prepositions used in a sentence and randomly replace them with different prepositions. The translation system should be least sensitive to this type of adversary because it typically results in the smallest change in the meaning of the sentence, as compared to switching the noun phrases.

3 Experiments

We use settings similar to that of Elliott (2018) in order to make the evaluation of textual adversaries comparable to that of visual adversaries. Each system in this analysis is trained on the 29,000 English-German-image triplets in the *translation* data in the Multi30K dataset (Elliott et al., 2016). The analysis is performed on the Multi30K Test

---

[1] The code to recreate these textual adversaries or new adversaries is available at `https://github.com/koeldc/Textual-adversaries-generation`

[2] The degree of concreteness in a word's context is correlated with the likelihood that the word is used in a literal sense and not metaphorically (Turney et al., 2011).

	Original	Visual	Textual			
			Num	Noun	NP	Prep
decinit	**51.5**	+0.4	-14.0	-11.1	-11.0	-5.7
trgmul	**52.1**	+0.2	-14.8	-11.2	-11.2	-5.8
hierattn	**48.2**	-2.0	-13.2	-9.4	-11.2	-5.4
Text-only	51.5	–	-14.6	-10.4	-10.5	-6.3

Table 1: The differences in Corpus-level Meteor scores for the English–German Multi30K Test 2017 data for the different adversaries compared to the systems evaluated on the Original text and images. Visual: evaluation on the correct text but adversarial images. Textual: evaluation on the four different textual adversaries and the correct images. Text-only: performance of a text-only translation model with adversarial sentences.

2017 split (Elliott et al., 2017). The predicted translations are evaluated against human references using Meteor 1.5 (Denkowski and Lavie, 2014). The translations of the sentences with textual adversaries are evaluated against the gold standard, and not what the model *should* predict, given the adversarial input.

In this analysis, we evaluate the performance of three off-the-shelf multimodal systems: **decinit** uses a learned transformation of a global 2048D visual feature vector is used to initialise the decoder hidden state (Caglayan et al., 2017a). In **trgmul**, the target language word embeddings and 2048D visual representations are interacted through element-wise multiplication (Caglayan et al., 2017a). In **hierattn**, the decoder learns to selectively attend to a combination of the source language and a $7{\times}7{\times}512$ volume of spatial-location preserving visual features (Libovický and Helcl, 2017). We also evaluate an attention-based text-only NMT system (Bahdanau et al., 2014) trained on only the English–German sentences in Multi30K. The model uses a conditional GRU decoder (Firat and Cho, 2016) with attention over a GRU encoder (Cho et al., 2014), as implemented in `nmtpytorch` (Caglayan et al., 2017b).

Visual Adversaries: Visual concepts and their relationships with the text are expected to provide rich supervision to multimodal translation systems. In addition to evaluating the robustness of these systems to textual adversaries, we also determine the interplay with visual adversaries. We pair each caption with a randomly sampled image from the test data to break the alignment between learned word semantics and visual concepts.

3.1 Results

In Table 1 we present the corpus-level Meteor scores for the text-only and multimodal systems when evaluated on the original data and the difference in performance when evaluating these models using the different adversaries. For visual adversaries, we confirm previously reported results of no substantial performance losses for the translations generated by the **trgmul** and **decinit** systems with visual features from unrelated images (Elliott, 2018). The **hierattn** model, however, is affected by the incongruent images, result in a 2.0 Meteor point drop in performance, indicating that the attention-based model is sensitive to the relevance of the visual input. In the case of the textual adversaries, all models suffer a significant drop in Meteor score for all types of adversary, with numeral replacements producing the largest differences. (This was a surprising result but we believe it is partially due to unseen numerals, e.g. "Seventeen" being mapped to the UNK token.) The **hierattn** model is least affected by noun and numeral replacements, and all three models are similarly affected by the noun phrase shuffle and prepositional swap adversaries. The text-only translation model is similarly affected by the textual adversaries, with the exception of the prepositional swap adversary, which has a more marked affect on performance than in the multimodal models.

In addition to the standard evaluation measures, we estimate the lexical diversity of the translations by calculating the type-to-token ratio (Templin, 1957, TTR) of the system outputs when evaluated with the congruent or incongruent visual inputs.[3]

---

[3]TTR has previously been used to estimate the quality of machine translation system outputs (Bentivogli et al., 2016).

	Congruent	Incongruent
decinit	0.1659	0.1655
trgmul	0.1703	0.1692
hierattn	0.1399	0.1352

Table 2: Type-to-token ratios of the system outputs given congruent and incongruent visual context.

	95 % Confidence Interval
Original	140.01 - 210.62
Num	335.03 - 490.07
Noun	388.02 - 511.52
NP	490.24 - 816.45
Prep	443.94 - 736.79

Table 3: The 95% confidence interval of the sentence-level perplexity of the original and each textual adversarial data samples, as estimated by GPT-2.

In our experiments, the multimodal systems were trained on the congruent image-sentence pairs so any difference in lexical diversity is likely to be due to the visual component of the respective models. However, the results in Table 2 indicate that there is no meaningful difference in TTR when the models are evaluated with the congruent or incongruent visual inputs.

3.2 Discussion

Given substantial decreases in Meteor score of the translations, we conducted an analysis to estimate the well-formedness of the adversarial sentences. To this end, we measure the perplexity of the perturbed sentences in each textual adversarial category using the pre-trained GPT-2 language model (Radford et al., 2018) and further average them to compute 95% confidence intervals for each category. From Table 3, we observe that the boundaries of the intervals are not over-lapping, indicating statistically significant differences in distribution between the adversarial categories and the original sample[4].

Qualitative Analysis: Figure 2 shows examples of translations under textual adversarial conditions for the **hierattn** system. We also show the output of the same system given the original text data. In these examples, we see that the system produces incorrect translations with respect to ei-

ther the sentence or the image. In NUM, pluralizing "A" to "Two" causes the model to generate an *unknown word*[5] "Japan" instead of "Halloween". The translation model is likely to have good representations of "A" and "two" because these words occur frequently in the training data, but it fails to distinguish between singulars and plurals, resulting in an incorrect translation. In PREP, swapping "in" for "up" causes the model to make an *incorrect lexical choice* "fische" ("fish") instead of "waterfall", which is incorrect, given the image. This example shows that a small lexical error can have a catastrophic effect on the output. This may be because the semantics of spatial relations are not diverse enough in Multi30K. In NOUN, replacing "man" with "city" causes the model to generate an output containing the *mistranslated unit* "Stadt"("city"), although a man is clearly visible in the image. This implies that addition visual signals is not always helpful in the obvious situations where we wish to translate direct visual terms. In NP, we see that the systems fail to fully capture the information contained in the image, resulting in *under-translation*. However, unlike the output in the adversarial condition, which did not translate the important visual concept "people", the model with the original sentence translates "People" into "Menschen". An inspection of the training data shows that there are sentences that describe 'people fishing', therefore the model may be exploiting the distribution in the training data.

Overall, this analysis shows that the visual modality does not help the system to recover the correct translation, given textual adversaries.

4 Conclusion

In this paper, we study the potential contribution of each modality for the task of multimodal machine translation. We evaluated the performance of three multimodal translations system with adversarial source language sentences that share some aspects of the correct caption. Our evaluation offers new insights on the limitations of these systems. The results indicate that the systems are primarily performing text-based translations, which is supported by the observation that the visual adversaries do not harm the systems as much as their textual counterparts. However, the textual adversaries sometimes resulted in ungrammatical sentences, which may be addressed by adopt-

---

[4]The higher perplexities for the adversarial samples were, in part, due to incorrect grammatical conjugations.

[5]We use the error taxonomy from Vilar et al. (2006).

Original: A group of young people dressed up for Halloween.
Baseline: Eine Gruppe junger Menschen verkleidet.
Num: <u>Two</u> groups of young people dressed up for halloween.
NMT: Zwei Frauen vor einem Glasgebäude.
MMT: Zwei Gruppen von jungen Menschen in Japan.
Reference : Eine Gruppe junger Leute verkleidet sich für Halloween.

Original: A man paddles an inflatable canoe.
Baseline: Ein Mann paddelt in einem aufblasbaren Kanu.
Noun: A <u>city</u> paddles an inflatable canoe.
NMT: Ein Bewölkter kissen über die Absperrung.
MMT: Eine Stadt paddelt in einem aufblasbaren Kanu.
Reference: Ein Mann paddelt in einem aufblasbaren Kanu.

Original: People fishing off a pier.
Baseline: Menschen beim Angeln.
NP: A <u>pier</u> fishing off <u>people</u>.
NMT: Ein Bewölkter kissen über die Absperrung.
MMT: Ein Pier beim Angeln.
Reference: Leute fischen an einem Pier.

Original: A beautiful waterfall in the middle of a forest.
Baseline: Ein schöner Wasserfall in der Mitte eines Waldes.
Prep: A beautiful waterfall <u>up</u> the middle of a forest.
NMT: Zwei Frauen vor einem Glasgebäude.
MMT: Eine schöne Fische in einem Wald.
Reference: Ein schöner Wasserfall mitten im Wald.

Figure 2: Examples of translations produced by the **hierattn** multimodal transaltion system. **Baseline**: the system output given the **Original** image-caption pair. Num / Noun / NP / Prep: The adversarial caption with the <u>underlined</u> replacement. **NMT**: the output of a text-only translation system, given the adversarial input. **MMT**: the output of the **hierattn** system, given the adversarial input.

ing recently-proposed neural perturbation models (Alzantot et al., 2018). We will also put more emphasis on the specific *visual term* in the image, aligning them with corresponding mention in the source data, and we plan on developing models with an max-margin ranking loss that forces the model to distinguish important differences (Huang et al., 2018) between the true image-sentence pair and well-formed adversarial perturbed sentences.

Acknowledgements

We thank Mareike Hartmann, Ákos Kádár, Mitja Nikolaus, Kai Pierre Waelti, Thiago Castro Ferreira and the reviewers for their feedback and comments on this paper.

References

Moustafa Alzantot, Yash Sharma, Ahmed Elgohary, Bo-Jhang Ho, Mani Srivastava, and Kai-Wei Chang. 2018. Generating natural language adversarial examples. In *Proceedings of the 2018 Conference on Empirical Methods in Natural Language Processing*, pages 2890–2896, Brussels, Belgium. Association for Computational Linguistics.

Dzmitry Bahdanau, Kyunghyun Cho, and Yoshua Bengio. 2014. Neural machine translation by jointly learning to align and translate. *arXiv preprint arXiv:1409.0473*.

Luisa Bentivogli, Arianna Bisazza, Mauro Cettolo, and Marcello Federico. 2016. Neural versus phrase-based machine translation quality: a case study. *arXiv preprint arXiv:1608.04631*.

Ozan Caglayan, Walid Aransa, Adrien Bardet, Mercedes García-Martínez, Fethi Bougares, Loïc Barrault, Marc Masana, Luis Herranz, and Joost Van de Weijer. 2017a. Lium-cvc submissions for wmt17 multimodal translation task. *arXiv preprint arXiv:1707.04481*.

Ozan Caglayan, Mercedes García-Martínez, Adrien Bardet, Walid Aransa, Fethi Bougares, and Loïc Barrault. 2017b. Nmtpy: A flexible toolkit for advanced neural machine translation systems. *Prague Bull. Math. Linguistics*, 109:15–28.

Ozan Caglayan, Pranava Madhyastha, Lucia Specia, and Loïc Barrault. 2019. Probing the need for visual context in multimodal machine translation. *arXiv preprint arXiv:1903.08678*.

Xinlei Chen, Hao Fang, Tsung-Yi Lin, Ramakrishna Vedantam, Saurabh Gupta, Piotr Dollár, and C Lawrence Zitnick. 2015. Microsoft coco captions: Data collection and evaluation server. *arXiv preprint arXiv:1504.00325*.

Kyunghyun Cho, Bart Van Merriënboer, Caglar Gulcehre, Dzmitry Bahdanau, Fethi Bougares, Holger Schwenk, and Yoshua Bengio. 2014. Learning phrase representations using rnn encoder-decoder for statistical machine translation. *arXiv preprint arXiv:1406.1078*.

Michael Denkowski and Alon Lavie. 2014. Meteor universal: Language specific translation evaluation for any target language. In *Proceedings of the ninth workshop on statistical machine translation*, pages 376–380.

Desmond Elliott. 2018. Adversarial evaluation of multimodal machine translation. In *Proceedings of the 2018 Conference on Empirical Methods in Natural Language Processing*, pages 2974–2978.

Desmond Elliott, Stella Frank, Loïc Barrault, Fethi Bougares, and Lucia Specia. 2017. Findings of the second shared task on multimodal machine translation and multilingual image description. In *Proceedings of the Second Conference on Machine Translation, Volume 2: Shared Task Papers*.

Desmond Elliott, Stella Frank, Khalil Sima'an, and Lucia Specia. 2016. Multi30k: Multilingual english-german image descriptions. *arXiv preprint arXiv:1605.00459*.

Orhan Firat and Kyunghyun Cho. 2016. Conditional gated recurrent unit with attention mechanism. *System BLEU baseline*, 31.

Stig-Arne Grönroos, Benoit Huet, Mikko Kurimo, Jorma Laaksonen, Bernard Merialdo, Phu Pham, Mats Sjöberg, Umut Sulubacak, Jörg Tiedemann, Raphael Troncy, et al. 2018. The memad submission to the wmt18 multimodal translation task. *arXiv preprint arXiv:1808.10802*.

Micah Hodosh and Julia Hockenmaier. 2016. Focused evaluation for image description with binary forced-choice tasks. In *Proceedings of the 5th Workshop on Vision and Language*, pages 19–28.

Matthew Honnibal and Mark Johnson. 2015. An improved non-monotonic transition system for dependency parsing. In *Proceedings of the 2015 Conference on Empirical Methods in Natural Language Processing*, pages 1373–1378.

Jiaji Huang, Yi Li, Wei Ping, and Liang Huang. 2018. Large margin neural language model. In *Proceedings of the 2018 Conference on Empirical Methods in Natural Language Processing*, pages 1183–1191.

Jindřich Libovický and Jindřich Helcl. 2017. Attention strategies for multi-source sequence-to-sequence learning. *arXiv preprint arXiv:1704.06567*.

George Miller. 1998. *WordNet: An electronic lexical database*. MIT press.

Alec Radford, Karthik Narasimhan, Tim Salimans, and Ilya Sutskever. 2018. Improving language understanding by generative pre-training.

Haoyue Shi, Jiayuan Mao, Tete Xiao, Yuning Jiang, and Jian Sun. 2018. Learning visually-grounded semantics from contrastive adversarial samples. *arXiv preprint arXiv:1806.10348*.

Lucia Specia, Stella Frank, Khalil Sima'an, and Desmond Elliott. 2016. A shared task on multimodal machine translation and crosslingual image description. In *Proceedings of the First Conference on Machine Translation: Volume 2, Shared Task Papers*, volume 2, pages 543–553.

Mildred C Templin. 1957. Certain language skills in children; their development and interrelationships.

Peter D Turney, Yair Neuman, Dan Assaf, and Yohai Cohen. 2011. Literal and metaphorical sense identification through concrete and abstract context. In *Proceedings of the Conference on Empirical Methods in Natural Language Processing*, pages 680–690. Association for Computational Linguistics.

David Vilar, Jia Xu, D'Haro Luis Fernando, and Hermann Ney. 2006. Error analysis of statistical machine translation output. In *LREC*, pages 697–702.

Peter Young, Alice Lai, Micah Hodosh, and Julia Hockenmaier. 2014. From image descriptions to visual denotations: New similarity metrics for semantic inference over event descriptions. *Transactions of the Association for Computational Linguistics*, 2:67–78.

Arnold M Zwicky. 1985. Heads. *Journal of linguistics*, 21(1):1–29.

Learning to Request Guidance in Emergent Communication

Benjamin Kolb[*] **Leon Lang**[*] **Henning Bartsch, Arwin Gansekoele,**
Raymond Koopmanschap, Leonardo Romor, David Speck, Mathijs Mul,[‡] **Elia Bruni**[†]

{benjamin.kolb, leon.lang, henning.bartsch,
arwin.gansekoele, raymond.koopmanschap, leonardo.romor,
david.speck, mathijs.mul}@student.uva.nl
elia.bruni@gmail.com

University of Amsterdam

Abstract

Previous research into agent communication has shown that a pre-trained guide can speed up the learning process of an imitation learning agent. The guide achieves this by providing the agent with discrete messages in an emerged language about how to solve the task. We extend this one-directional communication by a one-bit communication channel from the learner back to the guide: It is able to ask the guide for help, and we limit the guidance by penalizing the learner for these requests. During training, the agent learns to control this gate based on its current observation. We find that the amount of requested guidance decreases over time and guidance is requested in situations of high uncertainty. We investigate the agent's performance in cases of open and closed gates and discuss potential motives for the observed gating behavior.

1 Introduction

A long-term goal of AI is to develop agents that can help humans execute complex tasks in the real world. Since reward functions that are aligned with human intentions are hard to manually specify (Amodei and Clark, 2016), other approaches besides Reinforcement Learning are needed for creating agents that behave in the intended way. Among these are Reward Modeling (Leike et al., 2018) and Imitation Learning (Pomerleau, 1991), but, eventually, it would be useful if we could use natural language to transmit wishes to the agents.

Recently, Mul et al. (2019) made progress in this direction by showing how communication can be used to guide a learner in a gridworld environment. Using emergent discrete messages, the guide is able to speed up the learning process of the learner and to let it generalize across incrementally more difficult environments.

[*]Equal contributions
[†]Shared senior authorship

In this setting, the communication channel is completely one-way: in each time step, the guide transmits a message that may help the learner make its decisions. In reality, however, communication is more complex than that: the guidance may be expensive and it can, therefore, be beneficial to have more sparse messages. Furthermore, the learner may want to ask for clarification if something is unclear. Therefore, it would be worthwhile if there was a communication channel from the learner back to the guide. It is this interactive nature of communication that arguably is needed for more advanced AI systems (Mikolov et al., 2016).

In this paper, we equip the learner introduced by Mul et al. (2019) with a binary gate to indicate its need for guidance in each time step. A penalty for the use of guidance incentivizes a sparse usage of the gate. By analyzing the relationship between the learner's usage of the gate and a number of measures, we show that the learner indeed learns to ask for guidance in a smart and economical way.

2 Related Work

In this section we briefly lay out relevant work that relate to our approach on the dimensions of following language instructions, emergent communication and the interactions that emerge from guidance requests.

2.1 Following Language Instruction

In recent years, much research has been conducted in the field of following language instructions. Since language commands build a way to interact with agents and communicate information in an effective and human-interpretable way, the agent's processing and understanding of these commands is relevant for our project. Starting with manually engineered mappings (Winograd,

Proceedings of the Beyond Vision and LANguage: inTEgrating Real-world kNowledge (LANTERN), pages 41–50
Hong Kong, China, November 3, 2019. ©2019 Association for Computational Linguistics

1971), the currently most relevant grounded language acquisition methods focus on learning a parser to map linguistic input to its executable equivalent, i.e. action specifications using statistical models (Yu et al., 2018), (Kim and Mooney, 2012), (Artzi and Zettlemoyer, 2013), (Mei et al., 2016). In the BabyAI platform introduced by Chevalier-Boisvert et al. (2019) a synthetic "Baby Language" is used, which consists of a subset of English and whose semantics is generated by a context-free grammar (as opposed to instruction templates) and is easily understood by humans. They employ a single model to combine linguistic and visual information, similar to Misra et al. (2017). Our setup builds on Mul et al. (2019) who extend that platform with a guide, like Co-Reyes et al. (2018), that supplements the agent's information with iterative linguistic messages.

2.2 Emergent Communication

In order to benefit most from the guide, the agent would ideally communicate back, thus creating a multi-agent cooperation scenario. Recent research in this area investigates the emergence and usage of emergent language, e.g. in the context of referential games (Lazaridou et al., 2016). Furthermore, Mordatch and Abbeel (2018) show that multiple agents can develop a grounded compositional language to fulfill their tasks more effectively with spoken exchange. In our setup the emergent communication consists of discrete word tokens similar to Havrylov and Titov (2017). Jiang and Lu (2018) propose an attentional communication model to learn when communication is needed (and helpful), resulting in more effective (large-scale) multi-agent cooperation.

2.3 Guidance Requests

In prior work (Mul et al., 2019), guidance is given at every time step and the communication is one-way from guide to learner. We extend this approach by allowing a communication channel in the other direction. Here we survey work that uses similar requests for help.

Most similar to our work is Clouse (1997), where "Ask for help" is proposed: in this setting, an RL agent has one additional action with which it can signify to a "trainer" that it wants to receive help. The trainer then chooses the agent's action. Whether to ask for help is based on uncertainty about the highest action value. This is different from our setting in which the uncertainty

is only *implicitly* responsible for queries, as can be seen in Section 5. Kosoy (2019) studies the "Ask for help" setting theoretically and proves a regret bound for agents that act in infinite-horizon discounted MDPs and are able to delegate actions to an "advisor".

In Nguyen et al. (2019) there is a help-requesting policy π_{help} that can signify if the agent needs help. If this is the case, a guide answers with a language-based instruction of subgoals. Additionally, there is a budget that limits asking for help.

Also related is Werling et al. (2015), where structured prediction problems are considered: a sequence of words is received and each word is supposed to be mapped to a label. The system can query a crowd (as in crowd-sourcing) to obtain answers on specific words in the sequence. As in our case, querying the crowd is penalized by an additional loss.

In Krueger (2016), Schulze and Evans (2018), active reinforcement learning (ARL) is proposed: different from usual RL, the agent has to choose in each round if it *wants* to receive the reward that results from its action, which results in a constant query-cost $c > 0$. Note that in this setting, what is queried is feedback, whereas in our setting, the model queries guidance *prior* to making a decision. Active Reward Learning (Daniel et al., 2014) is a similar approach in the context of continuous control tasks.

3 Approach

3.1 BabyAI Game

All our experiments take place in the BabyAI platform (Chevalier-Boisvert et al., 2019). In this platform, an agent learns to complete tasks given by instructions in a subset of English in a mini grid-world environment. The environments are only partially observable to the agent.

Figure 1 shows two example levels. In total there are 19 different levels that increase in difficulty and complexity of tasks. For each level, the BabyAI framework can randomly generate many missions that require roughly the same skillset and are provided with a similar language instruction. For the following investigation, we only focus on the levels "GoToObj" and "PutNextLocal". These are chosen to be simple but nevertheless require a representative set of skills. As such, our results can be understood as a proof of concept.

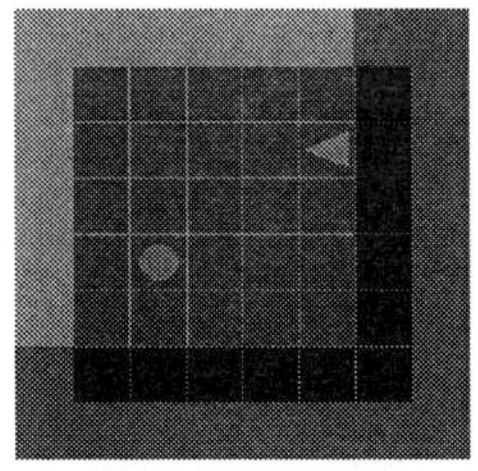
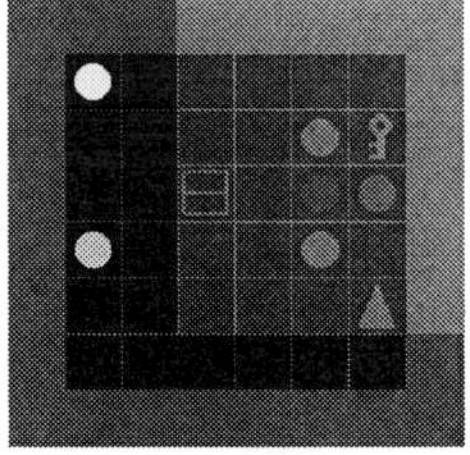

(a) GoToObj   (b) PutNextLocal

Figure 1: Example levels from BabyAI. GoToObj is the simplest level, requiring the agent to go to a specific object. This task is given by a language instruction to the agent, such as "Go to the purple ball". PutNextLocal is more difficult, requiring a more complex skill-set. An example task in this setting would be "Put the grey key next to the red box". Shown in the images are the agent (red triangle), different objects (boxes, keys, balls in different colors) and the observation of the agent (a brighter 7×7 visual field that has the agent in the middle of the bottom row relative to the agent. Parts of this is outside of the shown images)

3.2 Model

In this section, we describe the model that we use for a learner that may ask for guidance. We refer to Figure 2 for a visual explanation.

Based on the observation o_t, the instruction i and its own memory unit, the learner L builds a representation r_t:

$$r_t = L(o_t, i). \tag{1}$$

o_t is a $7 \times 7 \times 3$ tensor describing the viewable environment (e.g. the brighter area in Figure 1) and i is a natural language instruction (e.g. "Go to the purple ball"). The representation unit L uses a FiLM module (Perez et al., 2017) followed by a memory RNN.

First, consider a learner without guidance. In this setting it directly takes the representation r_t and feeds it into the policy module P that outputs the next action $a_t = P(r_t)$. For more details on this baseline setting, see Chevalier-Boisvert et al. (2019).

A guided learner

Now consider Mul et al. (2019), where a guide is added. The guide follows the same architecture as the learner-policy combination, but between the representing unit and the policy there is a discrete "bottleneck" that only allows 9 different messages to pass. The policy then needs to encode this message continuously in order to choose the correct

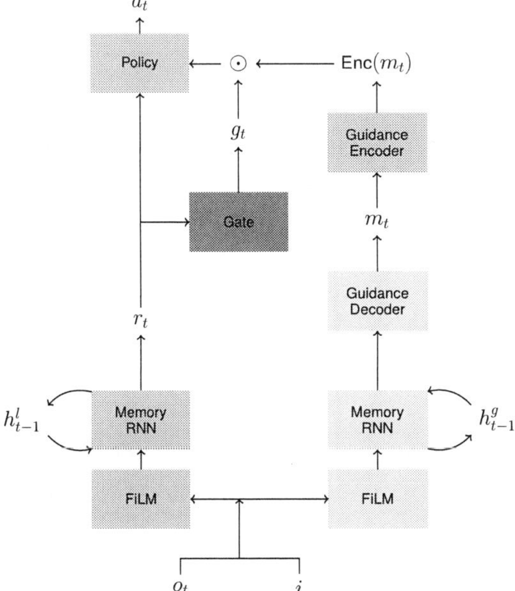

Figure 2: Architecture of a learner that can ask for guidance. Depicted variables are o_t: observation input, i: linguistic instruction, h^l_{t-1} and h^g_{t-1}: memory, r_t: learned representation, m_t: the discrete guidance message, g_t: the gating weight and a_t: the action chosen based on r_t and possibly the encoded message $\text{Enc}(m_t)$. The red part (the guide) is pretrained and then finetuned, while the blue parts (conceptually belonging to the learner) are newly initialized at the beginning of the training.

action out of 7 possibilities. After this guide-policy combination is trained, the messages are fed into the policy attached to a newly initialized learner in order to help it make its decision. In this later guided training stage, the policy of the guide is not used anymore.

More formally, the guide uses the same input and a memory unit to produce a message m_t of two words with 3 possible tokens for each.

$$m_t = G(o_t, i). \tag{2}$$

The message m_t is then encoded to a higher dimensional continuous encoding $\text{Enc}(m_t)$ that is produced by an encoder of the same architecture as the encoder used while training the guide. The policy then bases its decision on both the learned representation r_t and encoding $\text{Enc}(m_t)$, which are simply concatenated:

$$a_t = P(r_t, \text{Enc}(m_t)). \tag{3}$$

More details can be found in Mul et al. (2019).

Adding a gate

To enable the learner to decide when to receive guidance, we extend the learner with a gate module G to learn a gating weight $g_t \in \{0, 1\}$ that switches the policy input between $(r_t, \text{Enc}(m_t))$ (guided) and $(r_t, \mathbf{0})$ (unguided):

$$
\begin{aligned}
a_t &= P(r_t, g_t \cdot \text{Enc}(m_t)) \\
&= P\left((1 - g_t) \cdot (r_t, \mathbf{0}) + g_t \cdot (r_t, \text{Enc}(m_t))\right) \\
&= \begin{cases} P(r_t, \mathbf{0}), & \text{if } g_t = 0, \\ P(r_t, \text{Enc}(m_t)), & \text{if } g_t = 1, \end{cases}
\end{aligned}
\tag{4}
$$

where $g_t = G(r_t)$. The gate module G is a two-layered MLP with a tanh activation functions that outputs a scalar, followed by a sigmoid activation function and a threshold function with parameter 0.5. The module G that produces the gating weight will from here on be referred to as the gate.

3.3 Training

We use a pretrained Reinforcement Learning (RL) expert, trained as in Mul et al. (2019) and Chevalier-Boisvert et al. (2019) by proximal policy optimization (Schulman et al., 2017). After training, the expert is placed once in many missions in order to create training data containing the expert behavior. Using imitation learning as in Mul et al. (2019), we have a cross-entropy loss function L_{ce} that measures how much the distribution over actions given by the policy of our model deviates from the "correct" action of the RL expert.[1] Furthermore, we penalize the learner for asking for guidance by adding the gating weight to the loss and balance these incentives by a hyperparameter λ:

$$
L = L_{\text{ce}} + \lambda \cdot g. \tag{5}
$$

We use $\lambda = 0.3$ in all GoToObj experiments and 0.05 for PutNextLocal, values that were found by hyperparameter search. The combined model consisting of pre-trained guide, also trained by imitation learning as in Mul et al. (2019), and the newly initialized learner is then trained end-to-end by backpropagating the gradients to all the weights of the combined model. In order to pass the gradients also through the discrete gate G, we use the straight-through estimator (Bengio et al., 2013; Courbariaux et al., 2016). In order to allow the learner to learn the usefulness of the guidance at the beginning of training, we initialize G with a positive bias.

4 Experiments

In this section, we describe the experiments conducted in order to test the setting of a learner that queries the guide for help. In order to assess this, we train the combined model with $\lambda = 0.3$ for 7 runs on the simplest level, GoToObj, until convergence. In this level, the learner is instructed to go to a specific object. Results with $\lambda = 0.05$ for 7 runs on the level PutNextLocal can be found in Appendix B.

Performance and dynamics. First of all, we are interested in how our model performs compared to baselines. The first baseline is the learner on its own trained with imitation learning, which was the setting in Chevalier-Boisvert et al. (2019). The second baseline is the learner that receives guidance in each round without the need to query for it, which was studied in Mul et al. (2019). We expect that our model learns faster than the original learner model, due to its access to guidance, but slower than the guided learner without the gate, since it does not always receive guidance. The results can be found in Figure 3 (a), where we plot the success rate, i.e. portion of successfully completed episodes, during validation.

We monitor the average gating weight over epochs, which we call *guidance rate*, to inspect the usage of the gate over the course of the training. Furthermore, we compare the overall accuracy with the accuracy conditioned on the cases of an open or closed gate to assess the influence on performance. These metrics can be found in Figure 3 (b).[2]

Since the accuracy plots in Figure 3 (b) are solely correlational, we furthermore plot the validation accuracy for the case where we *intervene* during validation in the gate in order to have it opened or closed to assess the causal influence of the open gate on the accuracy, see Figure 4.

Economic requests. While the accuracy mea-

---

[1] For mitigating confusion, we mention explicitly that the RL expert is not the same as the guide: the expert creates the data that is used for backpropagating the model and thus for training it *following* the choice of the action. The guide, however, gives its guidance *prior to* the decision about the chosen action.

[2] The accuracy is the percentage of chosen actions that coincide with the "correct" action of the RL expert that is used in the imitation learning process.

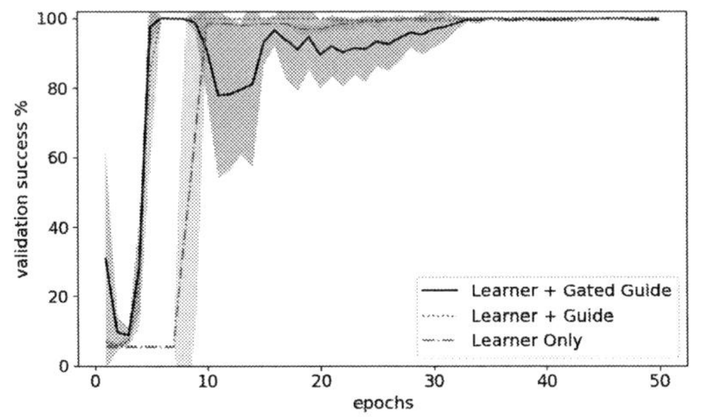

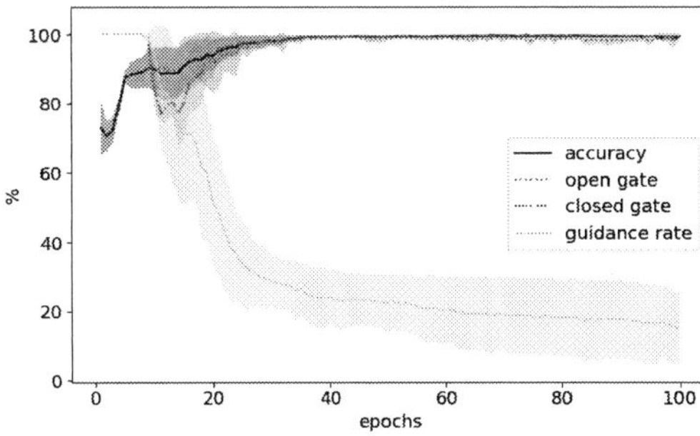

(a) Baseline Success Rate Comparison   (b) Validation Accuracy Comparison

Figure 3: Results of training our combined model until convergence on GoToObj. Results are averaged over 7 runs. Shaded regions represent standard deviations.

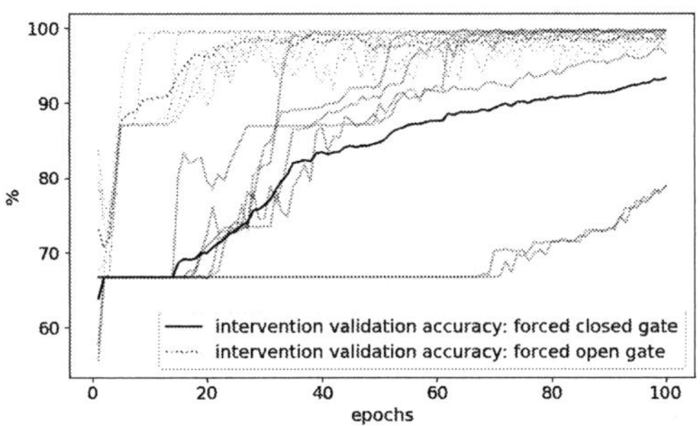

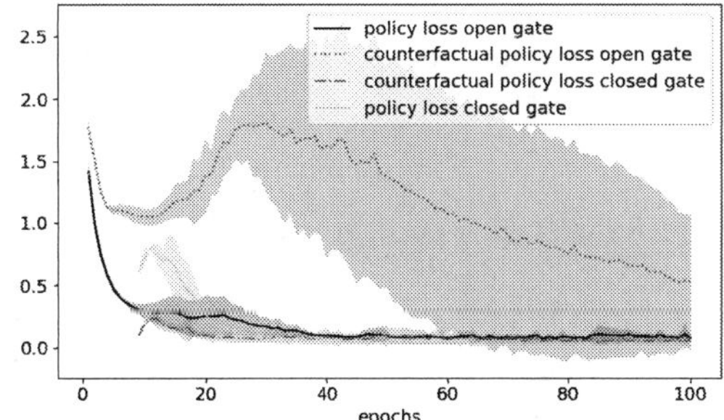

Figure 4: We compare the accuracy during validation in cases of forced open and closed gates: irrespective of the gating weight g_t computed from the system, we set $g_t = 1$ (so that the policy bases its decision on the encoded guidance $\text{Enc}(m_t)$) for the red dotted curve and $g_t = 0$ for the black curve.

Figure 5: Policy Loss Comparison

sures how often the agent was "right", the cross-entropy policy loss gives greater insights into the performance with respect to the actual training objective. We would like to assess whether the learner uses the gate economically, since it is penalized. This means to ask for guidance in situations in which it expects the greatest reduction in the policy loss. The policy loss for cases of open and closed gate can therefore be found in Figure 5. We compare it with the counterfactual policy losses that arise if we force the gate to be opened if the learner wants it to be closed and vice versa. This intervention now allows us to assess the *causal* influence of the gate on the policy loss.

Guidance semantics. Finally, we are interested in whether there are meaningful correlations between the frames in which the learner asks for guidance and the actions that the learner takes

(Figure 6) as well as the messages emitted by the guide (Figure 7). By analyzing this, we can see if the learner masters certain situations that require a certain action or are accompanied by a certain message.

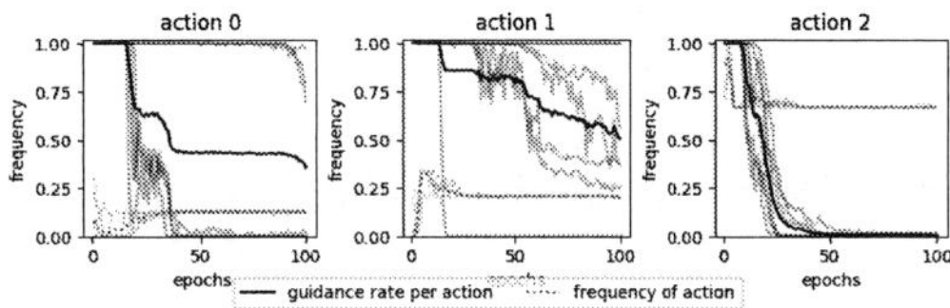

Figure 6: Frequency of open gate conditioned on actions and frequencies of actions themselves.

5 Analysis

5.1 Results and analysis of experiments

After outlining the experiments, we now briefly analyze the results.

Performance and dynamics. First, we notice in Figure 3 (a) that, while initially our model is

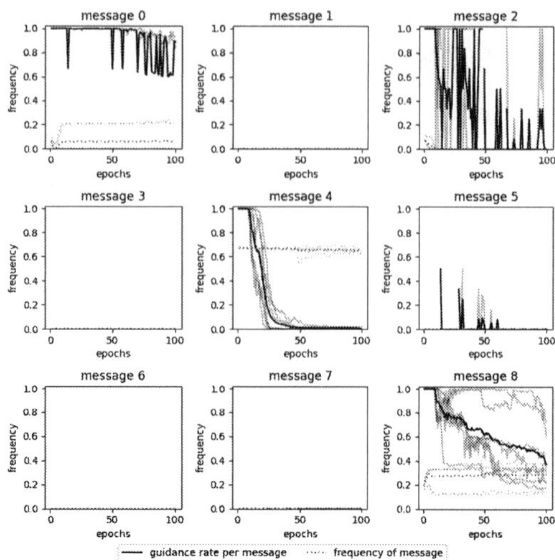

Figure 7: Frequency of open gate conditioned on messages and frequencies of messages themselves.

indeed faster than the learner baseline and keeps up with the guided baseline, from epoch 10 to 30 there is a performance dip not seen in the former models. This is precisely the phase in which the gate successively closes more and more, as can be seen in Figure 3 (b). Our explanation for this dip is that the policy first needs to adjust to the fact that it does not get the familiar guidance anymore. Eventually, from epoch 30 onward, our model performs almost perfectly and as well as the baselines.

As mentioned already, the learner becomes indeed more independent over time, roughly choosing its action on its own in 80% of the cases from epoch 50 onward. As soon as the guidance rate begins to drop in epoch 10, we can compute an accuracy conditioned on cases where the gate is closed, as can be seen in the blue line of Figure 3 (b). This accuracy is lower than the accuracy in case of an open gate (red dotted line) and only fully catches up roughly after 25 epochs of training.

About the intervention accuracy in Figure 4: we observe that the initial phase with a guidance rate at 1 sees a steep increase in accuracy with guidance but nearly no change in the accuracy without guidance. We suppose that is the case since in this phase the training happens exclusively with an open gate. Then, the guidance rate drops and training happens increasingly without guidance. Accordingly, the accuracy without guidance starts to increase and eventually catches up. In many individual runs, the performance without guidance

is ultimately actually even better. We hypothesize that this is since the gate is mostly closed and so the policy doesn't "expect" the gate to be open anymore. Consequently, an open gate and additional encoded message is confusing and leads to misbehavior. Intuitively, this is similar to how humans who are very experienced in their profession may actually just be distracted by someone who occasionally tries to give them advice instead of just letting them do their task on their own.

Economic requests. In order to get a better feeling for how smart the agent is in its guidance requests, we look at Figure 5. For similar results about the entropy, see Appendix A. We see an overall tendency for the policy loss to decrease, as we would expect due to the training. At the same time, the situations where the gate is open are those that are more difficult for the learner (including in the comparison of the counterfactual cases where we change the gate). Additionally, in those situations the reduction in policy loss achieved by asking for guidance is greater – this can be seen by comparing with the counterfactual situations. We furthermore observe that after the guidance rate starts to drop around epoch 10, the policy loss in situations of a closed gate rapidly sinks as the learner adapts to those novel situations. In the meantime, the open gate policy loss stabilizes until around epoch 20, while the counterfactual policy loss in these situations strongly increases. This indicates that the learner learns to selectively open the gate in situations that are more difficult and especially so without guidance.

Guidance semantics. To gain insights about dependencies between specific actions and the guidance rate, we now look at Figure 6. We see that in situations where the learner takes action 2, which corresponds to "move forward", the guidance rate drops relatively early to 0. This may be the case since this is the most common and supposedly most easily identifiable action. For action 0 that corresponds to "turn right" and action 1 that corresponds to "turn left", we see that the guidance rate also decreases, albeit slower and asymmetrically. This may be due to a higher difficulty of distinguishing those actions from each other. Intuitively they are symmetric and it may often be unclear what to do if "move forward" is not a promising action. In some runs, the guidance rate drops more for action 0 and in some more for action 1. We may attempt to explain this by the learner either learning to request help in situations where action 0 is one of the promising options (potentially the only one) or learning the same with action 1. In both cases, it is ensured that situations with confusion between those two actions are encompassed.

On the guidance rate conditioned on messages: as we can see in Figure 7, mainly three messages are used to convey guidance and for all of them the guidance rate decreases over time. We suppose that the overall trends happen due to the close correspondence between messages and actions that was already observed by Mul et al. (2019).

5.2 Guidance in space and time

So far, we mainly discussed "global" metrics, in the sense that we aggregate information over complete epochs. This still leaves open the question how guidance requests evolve with respect to the position of the agent and temporally during an episode.

For the first aim, we create heatmaps as in Figure 8. For more maps, see Figure 13 in Appendix A.

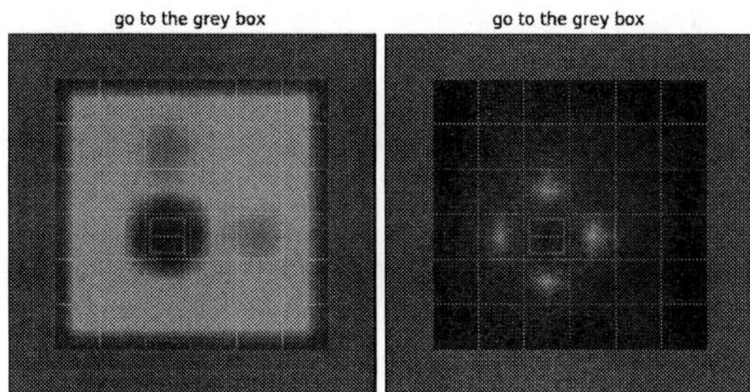

Figure 8: Two example heatmaps from training in level GoToObj, one in the beginning of training and one in an advanced stage. These heatmaps are created as follows: after an epoch is finished, the agent is placed in a specific mission. Then, we let it follow its path until the episode is over. For each point in the agent trajectory we record whether it asks for guidance. Multiple trajectories are sampled by randomly placing the agent in a new position. The brightness of the color in the figure depicts the average guidance rate within that position.

As we can see, the trained agent asks for guidance often specifically if it is near the goal object in order to find out if it should "turn towards it", which would cause the goal to be reached. It is important for the agent to be reasonably sure about the goal being reached beforehand, since otherwise turning to the object will result in two lost moves.

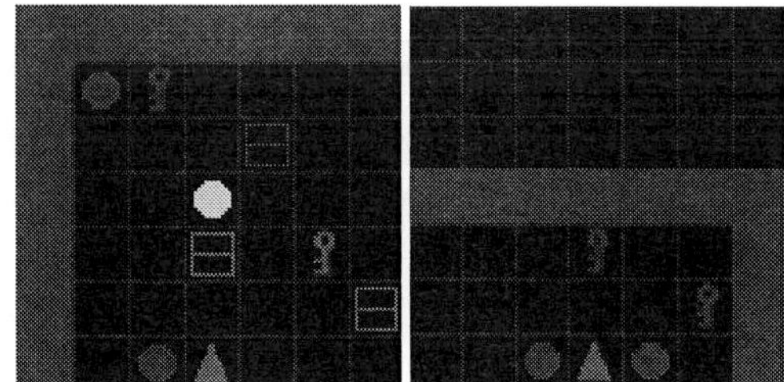

Figure 9: Observation types in GoToLocal. GoToLocal is a level different from GoToObj or PutNextLocal and is used to illustrate some of the extra possibilities $((1,x)$ and $(x,1))$ on further levels. In the left mission, the agent is tasked to go to the blue ball. This is directly left from the agent, whereas to the right, there is no feature in common with the goal. Therefore, the observation type is $(2,0)$. In the right mission, the goal is to go to a grey ball. Since the blue ball shares one feature with the grey one (namely being a ball), the corresponding observation type is $(1,2)$.

In order to test the influence of objects on the agent more quantitatively, we create another metric that conditions the guidance rate on how "goal-like" the observation is that the agent faces. For this matter, we assign tuples (d_1, d_2) to each observation, where d_1 and d_2 signify how goal-like the object left and right from the agent is. We measure this by the number of features it has in common with the goal object, where features are both color and object-type. $d_i = k$ means that the object shares $k \in \{0, 1, 2\}$ features with the goal object. This creates 9 observation types[3]. See Figure 9 for examples. The results can be found in Figure 10. We can observe strong changes in the guidance rate if the goal object is to the left or right: if it is on the left, the guidance rate is significantly greater and if it is to the right, the guidance rate is significantly smaller than usually. This is in line with the plots of the guidance rate conditioned on actions, Figure 6, which already showed that turning to the left requires considerably more guidance than turning to the right. This indicates that the high guidance rate at goal objects may to a large extend be caused by the high correlation between turning actions and guidance rates and be mostly independent of the fact that there is a goal

---

[3]Note that even the combination $(2, 2)$ is in principle possible in higher levels: There are tasks such as "Go to a red ball" where several red ball can be in the mission. However, this is unlikely and the expert never places itself between two goal objects. Furthermore, in GoToObj there is simply just one object in the mission. Therefore, the graph in Figure 10 corresponding to $(2, 2)$ is empty.

around.

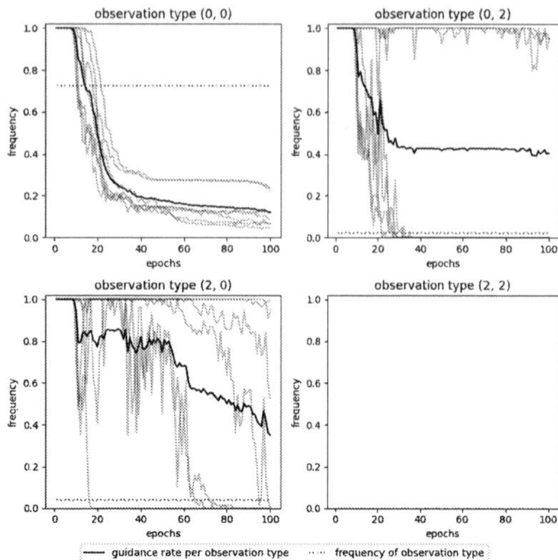

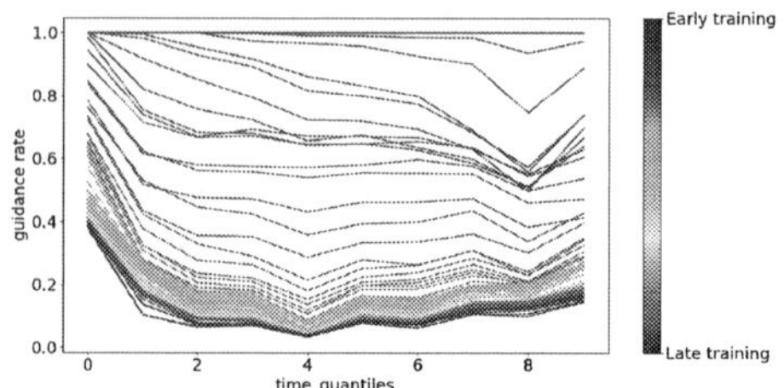

Figure 11: Guidance per time quantile: roughly speaking, a timepoint t is in quantile k of 10 if $t/l \approx k/10$, where l is the length of the corresponding episode. The plots show the guidance rate corresponding to the different quantiles. Dark blue curves belong to earlier epochs whereas red curves belong to later epochs.

Figure 10: Frequency of open gate conditioned on observation types and frequencies of observation types themselves. For example, type $(2, 0)$ is a situation where directly left of the agent there is the goal and right of it there is no object sharing any feature with the goal-object. In GoToObj there is only one object in the level so situations like $(1, x)$ or $(x, 1)$ do not occur and are left out in this plot.

Now we turn to the question about the guidance rate in time: within one episode, are there usually phases where more or less guidance is needed? The heatmaps suggest that the agent mostly asks for guidance in the end of the episode.

In order to answer this question, we create the "guidance per time quantile" plot, Figure 11. As we can see, the guidance rate is in general high in the beginning of episodes and drops once more knowledge about the environment is acquired. However, in the end of the episode, the guidance rate grows again and is greatest in the very end, which is in line with the qualitative assessment from the heatmaps.

One interpretation for this is the following: in the beginning, the agent needs to roughly figure out "in which direction to head". Once this is clear, it can walk there without further guidance. But in the very end, it needs more precision and asks for guidance again in order to finally find its goal. This is similar to how humans often look at a map in the beginning of a hike in order to figure out the direction, and then in the end again in order to reassess how their new position now relates to the goal.

6 Conclusion and future research

In this paper, we extended a recently proposed method to guide a learner in a gridworld environment by letting the learner explicitly ask for help. To accomplish this, we defined a binary gate in the learner's model. We brought the original approach closer to the real world by (i) enabling bi-directional communication and (ii) attaching a cost to it.

We showed that the learner successfully learns to utilize the guidance gate to achieve a favorable trade-off between learning speed and amount of guidance requested. Initially using the full guidance to learn faster than a learner without guidance, it eventually learns to request guidance only where it is especially helpful, acting increasingly independent.

Future research could consist of retraining the guide to see if it learns to send more abstract messages that provide guidance over multiple time steps. This may be fruitfully combined with giving the guide an additional information advantage like a bird's eye's view so that the guide has more foresight than the learner. It would require a way for the learner to memorize past messages.

Another direction is to replace the gate by an emergent communication channel from the learner to the guide, so that the learner can send its guidance requests in more nuanced ways. Furthermore, we saw that the policy may have problems dealing with the additional guidance it receives unexpectedly in late training. It may be worthwhile to experiment with policy architectures that can deal better with spontaneous changes in its input.

Finally, research might as well aim at finding ways to meaningfully replace the guide agent by a human. This might allow for better learning in tasks that autonomous agents struggle to learn by themselves.

References

Dario Amodei and Jack Clark. 2016. Faulty reward functions in the wild. https://openai.com/blog/faulty-reward-functions/. Accessed: 2019-06-22.

Yoav Artzi and Luke Zettlemoyer. 2013. Weakly supervised learning of semantic parsers for mapping instructions to actions. *Transactions of the Association for Computational Linguistics*, 1:49–62.

Yoshua Bengio, Nicholas Léonard, and Aaron Courville. 2013. Estimating or propagating gradients through stochastic neurons for conditional computation. *arXiv preprint arXiv:1308.3432*.

Maxime Chevalier-Boisvert, Dzmitry Bahdanau, Salem Lahlou, Lucas Willems, Chitwan Saharia, Thien Huu Nguyen, and Yoshua Bengio. 2019. BabyAI: First steps towards grounded language learning with a human in the loop. In *International Conference on Learning Representations*.

J. Clouse. 1997. On integrating apprentice learning and reinforcement learning title2:. Technical report, Amherst, MA, USA.

John D Co-Reyes, Abhishek Gupta, Suvansh Sanjeev, Nick Altieri, John DeNero, Pieter Abbeel, and Sergey Levine. 2018. Guiding policies with language via meta-learning. *arXiv preprint arXiv:1811.07882*.

Matthieu Courbariaux, Itay Hubara, Daniel Soudry, Ran El-Yaniv, and Y Bengio. 2016. Binarized neural networks: Training deep neural networks with weights and activations constrained to +1 or -1.

C. Daniel, M. Viering, J. Metz, O. Kroemer, and J. Peters. 2014. Active reward learning. In *Proceedings of Robotics: Science & Systems*.

Serhii Havrylov and Ivan Titov. 2017. Emergence of language with multi-agent games: Learning to communicate with sequences of symbols. In *Advances in neural information processing systems*, pages 2149–2159.

Jiechuan Jiang and Zongqing Lu. 2018. Learning attentional communication for multi-agent cooperation. In *Advances in Neural Information Processing Systems*, pages 7254–7264.

Joohyun Kim and Raymond J Mooney. 2012. Unsupervised pcfg induction for grounded language learning with highly ambiguous supervision. In *Proceedings of the 2012 Joint Conference on Empirical Methods in Natural Language Processing and Computational Natural Language Learning*, pages 433–444. Association for Computational Linguistics.

Vanessa Kosoy. 2019. Delegative reinforcement learning: learning to avoid traps with a little help. *Safe Machine Learning workshop at ICLR*.

David Krueger. 2016. Active reinforcement learning : Observing rewards at a cost.

Angeliki Lazaridou, Alexander Peysakhovich, and Marco Baroni. 2016. Multi-agent cooperation and the emergence of (natural) language. *arXiv preprint arXiv:1612.07182*.

Jan Leike, David Krueger, Tom Everitt, Miljan Martic, Vishal Maini, and Shane Legg. 2018. Scalable agent alignment via reward modeling: a research direction. *CoRR*, abs/1811.07871.

Hongyuan Mei, Mohit Bansal, and Matthew R Walter. 2016. Listen, attend, and walk: Neural mapping of navigational instructions to action sequences. In *Thirtieth AAAI Conference on Artificial Intelligence*.

Tomas Mikolov, Armand Joulin, and Marco Baroni. 2016. A roadmap towards machine intelligence.

Dipendra Misra, John Langford, and Yoav Artzi. 2017. Mapping instructions and visual observations to actions with reinforcement learning. *arXiv preprint arXiv:1704.08795*.

Igor Mordatch and Pieter Abbeel. 2018. Emergence of grounded compositional language in multi-agent populations. In *Thirty-Second AAAI Conference on Artificial Intelligence*.

Mathijs Mul, Diane Bouchacourt, and Elia Bruni. 2019. Mastering emergent language: learning to guide in simulated navigation. *arXiv e-prints*, page arXiv:1908.05135.

Khanh Nguyen, Debadeepta Dey, Chris Brockett, and Bill Dolan. 2019. Vision-based navigation with language-based assistance via imitation learning with indirect intervention. In *Proceedings of the IEEE Conference on Computer Vision and Pattern Recognition*, pages 12527–12537.

Ethan Perez, Florian Strub, Harm de Vries, Vincent Dumoulin, and Aaron Courville. 2017. Film: Visual reasoning with a general conditioning layer.

Dean A. Pomerleau. 1991. Efficient training of artificial neural networks for autonomous navigation. *Neural Computation*, 3:97.

John Schulman, Filip Wolski, Prafulla Dhariwal, Alec Radford, and Oleg Klimov. 2017. Proximal policy optimization algorithms. *ArXiv*, abs/1707.06347.

Sebastian Schulze and Owain Evans. 2018. Active reinforcement learning with monte-carlo tree search. *CoRR*, abs/1803.04926.

Keenon Werling, Arun Tejasvi Chaganty, Percy S
Liang, and Christopher D Manning. 2015. On-
the-job learning with bayesian decision theory. In
C. Cortes, N. D. Lawrence, D. D. Lee, M. Sugiyama,
and R. Garnett, editors, *Advances in Neural Information Processing Systems 28*, pages 3465–3473.
Curran Associates, Inc.

Terry Winograd. 1971. Procedures as a representation for data in a computer program for understanding natural language. Technical report, MAS-
SACHUSETTS INST OF TECH CAMBRIDGE
PROJECT MAC.

Haonan Yu, Haichao Zhang, and Wei Xu. 2018. Interactive grounded language acquisition and generalization in a 2d world. *arXiv preprint
arXiv:1802.01433*.

At a Glance: The Impact of Gaze Aggregation Views on Syntactic Tagging

Sigrid Klerke
Department of Computer Science
ITU Copenhagen, Denmark
sigridklerke@gmail.com

Barbara Plank
Department of Computer Science
ITU Copenhagen, Denmark
bplank@itu.dk

Abstract

Readers' eye movements used as part of the training signal have been shown to improve performance in a wide range of Natural Language Processing (NLP) tasks. Previous work uses gaze data either at the type level or at the token level and mostly from a single eye-tracking corpus. In this paper, we analyze type vs token-level integration options with eye tracking data from two corpora to inform two syntactic sequence labeling problems: binary phrase chunking and part-of-speech tagging. We show that using globally-aggregated measures that capture the central tendency or variability of gaze data is more beneficial than proposed local views which retain individual participant information. While gaze data is informative for supervised POS tagging, which complements previous findings on unsupervised POS induction, almost no improvement is obtained for binary phrase chunking, except for a single specific setup. Hence, caution is warranted when using gaze data as signal for NLP, as no single view is robust over tasks, modeling choice and gaze corpus.

1 Introduction

Digital traces of human cognitive processing can provide valuable signal for Natural Language Processing (Klerke et al., 2016; Plank, 2016a,b). One emerging source of information studied within NLP is eye-tracking data (Barrett and Søgaard, 2015a; Klerke et al., 2016; Mishra et al., 2017a; Jaffe et al., 2018; Barrett et al., 2018b; Hollenstein et al., 2019). While ubiquitous gaze recording remains unavailable, NLP research has focused on exploring the value of including gaze information from large, mostly disjointly labeled gaze datasets in recurrent neural network models. This models the assumption that no new gaze data will be available at test time. The proposed approaches under this paradigm include gaze as auxiliary task

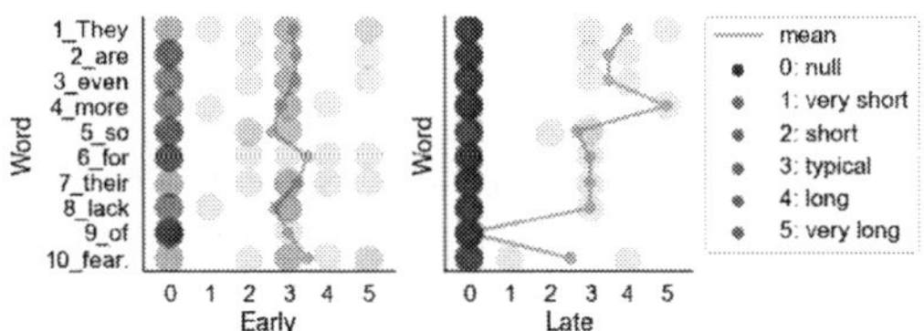

Figure 1: Gaze (binned) captured during reading.

in multi-task learning (Klerke et al., 2016; Hollenstein et al., 2019), gaze as word embeddings (Barrett et al., 2018b), gaze as type dictionaries (Barrett et al., 2016; Hollenstein and Zhang, 2019) and as attention (Barrett et al., 2018a). We follow this line of work and require no gaze data at test time.

Choosing a gaze representation means choosing what to consider as signal and what to consider as noise. Aggregation is a way to implement this choice; where the kind of aggregation typically depends on the modeling framework. In this work we investigate how different levels of aggregation and the kind of variability preserved in representations of gaze duration from early and late processing states interact with two low-level syntactic sequence labeling tasks. Specifically, we address the following questions:

RQ1 Is a *local* view of individual gaze trace beneficial for syntactic sequence labeling in comparison to an aggregate *global* view, where information is traced via i) the central tendency (mean) or ii) the variability (variance) of the gaze behavior?

RQ2 How well does learning from de-contextualized gaze data represented at the *type*-level (as dictionary) perform in comparison to learning from contextualized gaze data, represented at the *token*-level (via multi-task learning)?

Proceedings of the Beyond Vision and LANguage: inTEgrating Real-world kNowledge (LANTERN), pages 51–61
Hong Kong, China, November 3, 2019. ©2019 Association for Computational Linguistics

Contribution The main contribution of this paper is to provide a systematic overview of the influence of two independent levels of gaze data aggregation on low-level syntactic labeling tasks at two separate levels of complexity; i.e., a simple chunk boundary tagging and a supervised POS-tagging task.

Our results support the claim that learning from gaze information under maximal (global) aggregation is more helpful than learning from less aggregated gaze representations across two corpora, two gaze metrics and two modelling setups.

However, we find that caution is warranted, as no single view, model or even gaze corpus show consistent improvement and the influence of single measures is not robust enough to identify a reliably helpful configuration for practical applications under the explored setups.

2 Background and Motivation

Eye movements during reading consist of fixations which are short stationary glances on individual words. These are interrupted by saccades, which are the ballistic movements between fixations. The gaze loosely traces the sequence of words in a text and gaze research in reading has at its basis the understanding that deviations from a monotone eye movement progression tend to occur when the reader's cognitive processing is being challenged by the text.

The raw gaze signal is a time series of (x, y)-coordinates mapped to word positons on the screen and clustered into consecutive fixations. This data must necessarily be pre-processed and radically filtered to fit the shape of any NLP problem (Holmqvist et al., 2011). NLP researchers therefore need to decide how to meaningfully aggregate and filter gaze corpora in order to construct a mapping of the time series onto the meaningful unit of the problem at hand, such as a sequence of words or sentences.

The most commonly applied feature extraction approach is based on counting durations of fixations, visits and re-visits per word as pioneered in the psycholinguistic tradition and most commonly aggregating to the global mean across multiple readers (see orange line in Figure 1).

An alternative paradigm to psycholinguistics-based feature extraction is to instead represent raw recorded scanpaths over entire word sequences as 2D or 3D matrices and images (von der Malsburg

et al., 2012; Martínez-Gómez et al., 2012; Benfatto et al., 2016; Mishra et al., 2017a). However, this paradigm has only been explored in a jointly labeled setting where gaze data is assumed to be available at test time. This requirement can not yet be met in most practical NLP-applications.

Positive results have emerged from a range of diverging representations. In some cases, including tens of gaze features show a benefit (Mishra et al., 2017a; Barrett and Søgaard, 2015b) while other studies report successful experiments using a single gaze feature (Barrett et al., 2018a; Klerke et al., 2016).

The extraction of multiple features from the same bit of a raw recording can in theory allow to represent multiple distinct views on the same data; the number of visits, the order of visits and the durations of visits are examples of distinct perspectives. However, when features partially or entirely subsume other features[1] the inclusion of multiple views effectively performs a complex implicit weighting of the available gaze information through partial duplication. In order to eliminate these subtle effects, this work follow the single-metric approach, using a strict split of the recorded fixation durations into an Early and a Late measure with no overlap (see Section 4 for details). This allows us to isolate the target dimensions of inquiry, namely *effects of the level of aggregation*.

The two candidate gaze metrics used in this work are the first pass fixation duration as our Early metric and regression duration for our Late metric, which are the same two metrics as employed for sentence compression by Klerke et al. (2016). While they studied only a multi-task learning setup and one level of aggregation, we focus on multiple levels of aggregation and two NLP tasks.

The latter study represents a group of studies where individual readers' records are available at training time (i.e., multiple copies of the data with annotations obtained from different reading behaviour) rather than learning from the aggregate of multiple readers. This approach which involves a minimal level of aggregation is frequently applied where individual readers' cognition is of primary interest, such as categorizing individual language skill level or behaviour (Martínez-Gómez et al., 2012; Matthies and Søgaard, 2013;

---

[1]E.g. total reading time subsumes first pass reading time entirely.

Augereau et al., 2016; Bingel et al., 2018). Noticeably, the opposite approach of using maximally aggregated type-level representations which average all readings across all occurrences and all participants, has also been shown to contribute to improvements (Barrett et al., 2016; Bingel et al., 2018; Hollenstein et al., 2019). The effect of these two different views (global vs local) on the same task hence remained unexplored and is a gap we seek to fill in this paper.

We focus on the use of gaze for syntax-oriented NLP tasks, because human readers' eye movements reflect necessary language processing work, including syntax parsing, to reach comprehension of a text[2] (Rayner et al., 2006; Demberg and Keller, 2008). Multiple concurrent triggers within the reader as well as within the text may affect unconscious eye movement planning and execution. For this reason, psycholinguistic research favors maximal averaging, seeking to eliminate as much noise as possible. In contrast, NLP-systems primarily suffer from, and seek to handle, specific hard cases. This indicates that the variability in the gaze signal is valuable to retain for learning patterns in the data for disambiguation.

To answer the research questions, we first split the gaze duration data into an Early and a Late measure which form two distinct views of the gaze data. We operationalize between-subject variation as a local and a global aggregate as described in Section 4. We then relate gaze variation to the token and type-level context-modeling distinction afforded with a multi-task learning setup and a type dictionary setup, respectively, as detailed in Section 3. We evaluate on both a simplified and a typical low-level syntactic sequence labeling task described in Section 5. Finally we report our results and draw perspectives to related work in Sections 6 and 7 and conclude.

3 Token and type modelling – as multi-task learning and dictionary supervision

We contrast the impact of learning from token-level gaze information with learning from a type-level aggregated representation. A compelling argument for the token-level representation is that preserving context-specific information may allow a model to distinguish words and contexts which elicit more and less predictable gaze behavior. However, direct comparisons have demonstrated that the type-level global mean, which discards information on ambiguity, may be preferable (Barrett et al., 2016; Hollenstein and Zhang, 2019), which is somewhat surprising as the tasks require token-level disambiguation. Hence, we test this distinction for several aggregation ways and corpora, to shed more light on this modeling choice. The following describes the neural network modelling options which allow this comparison.

Multi-task learning (MTL) trains a neural network model to predict gaze data as an auxiliary task to the target task (Caruana, 1997). At training time, an input sentence is drawn from one of the task specific training sets. The relevant output is evaluated against the gold labeling and if a loss is recorded, parameters are updated accordingly. By forcing the two tasks to share parameters, the gaze information floats into the shared parameters through back-propagation. In this way, updates caused by losses on one task affect the activations and output on the other task.

Dictionary modelling trains a neural network model on a target task where the base representation of each word of an input sentence is concatenated with type-level gaze-derived features stored as a separate set of word embeddings, as further detailed in Section 5.2.

4 Eye-tracking Data

We extract gaze data from two large-scale eye-tracking corpora, the English part of the Dundee corpus (Kennedy et al., 2003) and the monolingual English reading part of the Ghent Eye-Tracking Corpus (GECO)[3] (Cop et al., 2017). Statistics of the corpora are provided in Table 1. The GECO corpus is more recent and contains more tokens (and utterances). The average sentence length is shorter compared to the Dundee corpus.

We use the English portion of the Dundee corpus which consists of recordings of 10 native English speakers' reading of 20 newspaper articles from *The Independent*. The text was presented for self-paced reading on a screen with a maximum of 5 lines at a time. The experimental setup included a set of comprehension questions after each article, re-calibration at every three screens and a

---

[2]For other tasks, non-linguistic aspects such as the reader's personal interest or emotional response to the reading material may be a primary argument for using gaze data.

[3] `http://expsy.ugent.be/downloads/geco/`

	GECO		Dundee	
Genre:	novel		news	
Readers:	14		10	
	Sents	Tokens	Sents	Tokens
Train	4,200	45,004	1,896	41,618
Dev	547	5,614	231	5,176
Test	574	5,792	243	5,206
Types	–	11,084	–	8,608

Table 1: Overview of the eye-tracking corpora. Type information is extracted from the training partition using the original white-space tokenization.

chin rest and bite bar to fixate head position during reading (Kennedy and Pynte, 2005). The extraction of our Early and Late metric use the original white-space tokenisation.[4]

From the GECO corpus we use the English monolingual reading data. This portion consists of recordings of 14 native English speakers' reading of the full novel *The Mysterious Affair at Styles* (Christie, 1920). The text was presented for self-paced reading on a screen with one paragraph or a maximum of 145 characters at a time. The novel was read in four sessions with comprehension questions and breaks after each chapter. Re-calibration was performed every 10 minutes or when drift was detected. The extraction of first pass duration is the `WORD_SELECTIVE_GO_PAST_TIME` feature in the published data and total regression duration is calculated as the total reading time from the feature `WORD_TOTAL_READING_TIME` minus the first pass duration.

No official train–dev–test split has been established for the corpora. We use the split of the Dundee corpus provided by Barrett et al. (2016): a training set containing 46,879 tokens/1,896 sentences, a development set containing 5,868 tokens/230 sentences, and a test set of 5,832 tokens/241 sentences. For GECO, we reserve the first and the last of every ten paragraphs as test and development sets, respectively.

4.1 Early and Late measures

For our Early metric of gaze processing we extract first pass fixation duration which is the total time spent looking on a word when it is first en-

---

countered, and be fore any subsequent words have been fixated, as the reader's gaze passes over the text. First pass duration may consist of several fixations accumulated up until the gaze leaves the word for the first time. When words are occasionally skipped on the first pass, null-values occur in the Early measure.

For our Late measure we use regression duration which is defined as the total time spent looking at the word on all later passes. We compute it as the total fixation time on the word minus the first pass duration, our Early measure. All words that were visited at most once will receive null values for this measure. These two metrics effectively split the total recorded reading time at every word with no overlap.

The duration measures are recorded in milliseconds with a minimum value defined by the lower fixation detection threshold as defined in the in the recording software (most commonly 40-50ms). This built-in offset and the reading speed variation between slow and fast readers, means that comparable relative variation (e.g., doubling in reading speed) within different readers contribute with different weight to the raw measure. In order to represent relative changes in reading speed consistently we standardize the raw durations of both metrics to each individual's average duration for each measure without counting null-values.

The standardization translates the raw measures into a record of how far a recorded duration on a given word is from the reader's typical time per word, expressed in standard deviations. Once standardized, the values are aggregated as described next.

4.2 Global and local views

As detailed in Section 2, Klerke et al. (2016) used each individual's gaze record as representation, which is a minimally aggregated gaze representation view that preserves the full width of participant's individual measures. Drawing from this view, we include a similar *local* view of the data. The local view collects the set of observed values for each type as a dictionary.

In contrast, the global view aggregates over the readings of all individuals. In particular, while the commonly-used mean is an estimate of a central tendency and produces a smoothed aggregate, variance is an estimate of how well the mean models the data and this measure is particularly sensitive to outliers. We use these two aggregates as *global* views; one representing a hypothetical typical reader; our other novel aggregate is representing the extent to which the eye movements of multiple readers agreed on an underlying sample.

4.3 Binning

The local and global measures are split into 6 distinct categorical bins following Klerke et al. (2016) and outlined below. One bin is reserved for the *null* values while the central standard deviation is considered the *typical* duration and an additional half of a standard deviation on each side denotes *short* and *long* duration spans. Values outside the central two standard deviations are binned as *very short* and *very long*, respectively.

0. $x = null$, not seen.
1. $x < -1$ SD, very short duration.
2. -1 SD $\leq x < -0.5$ SD, short duration.
3. -0.5 SD $\leq x < 0.5$ SD, typical duration.
4. 0.5 SD $\leq x < 1$ SD, long duration.
5. 1 SD $\leq x$, very long duration.

The binned values assigned for two example sentences from each corpus are shown in Figure 2a–2d. Each subject's (local) Early and Late measures are shown as a translucent large dot: several dots in the same category are represented as darker dots, and between-subject mean (global) is included as small connected orange dots. The null values (purple) are not included in the global aggregate. Practically, this decision means that as long as a single participant spend time fixating or re-fixating a word, the information about any participants who do not spend time on this particular word is lost in the global aggregates.

Inspecting the figure reveals how the Early measure is the most variable: we observe many grey dots per word, and fewer words with no attention on first pass (pale purple dots). In contrast, the Late measure is frequently recorded as null, reflecting how most words are not revisited. Interestingly, the GECO data (right figures), even though it has more (14) participants, noticeably it shows more agreement and less spread of the Late measure compared to the Dundee data. This difference may be attributable to the difference in text genre, readability, reading task formulation or sample differences.[5]

The robust effects of word length, frequency and wrap-up are discernible in the examples shown in Figure 2. Specifically, long words such as "visiting" in Figure 2c and the sentence boundary for example at the end of Figure 2d have received more attention than surrounding words. The wrap-up effect occur at boundaries of syntactically meaningful units and mostly reflects the time needed for the cognitive processing to catch up to the eyes (Rayner, 1998).

5 Experiments

Our experiments focus on two levels of syntactic influence on gaze data. In order to leverage the wrap-up effect, we design a simplified chunk boundary detection task, modelled as a binary sequence labeling problem. The second task is the classic supervised POS-tagging task.

5.1 Data

Chunking data The chunk boundary data was extracted from the CoNLL2000 chunking data (Sang and Buchholz, 2000) which consists of 8,936 training sentences. Punctuation is not treated as separate tokens in gaze data, which is why we augment the CoNLL2000 data by combining punctuation with any preceding character and dropping its label. To isolate the boundary detection problem, we retain only the chunk prefixes B and I. That is, 315 distinct tokens were labeled O originally. Of these, O-labeled coordinating conjunctions were found in 2,803 sentences. We re-label these as B, positing that these conjunctions act as unary chunks between the boundaries of existing chunks. We proceed to drop all remaining sentences with any remaining O-labels, which leaves a dataset of 8,204 sentences, 91,8% of the original sentences. The new binary labels show a slightly un-balanced label distribution of 58.8% tokens labeled B. The test set after binarization has 1881 sentences corresponding to 93.5% of the original test set with the label B accounting for 58.5% of the tokens.

POS data We use the English part of the Universal Dependencies (UD version 2.1) POS tagging data built over the source material of the English Web Treebank.[6] The tagset spans the 17 universal POS tags. We use the standard splits provided

---

[5]The more recent GECO sample population is likely more accustomed to screen reading

[6]`https://github.com/`
`UniversalDependencies/UD_English-EWT`

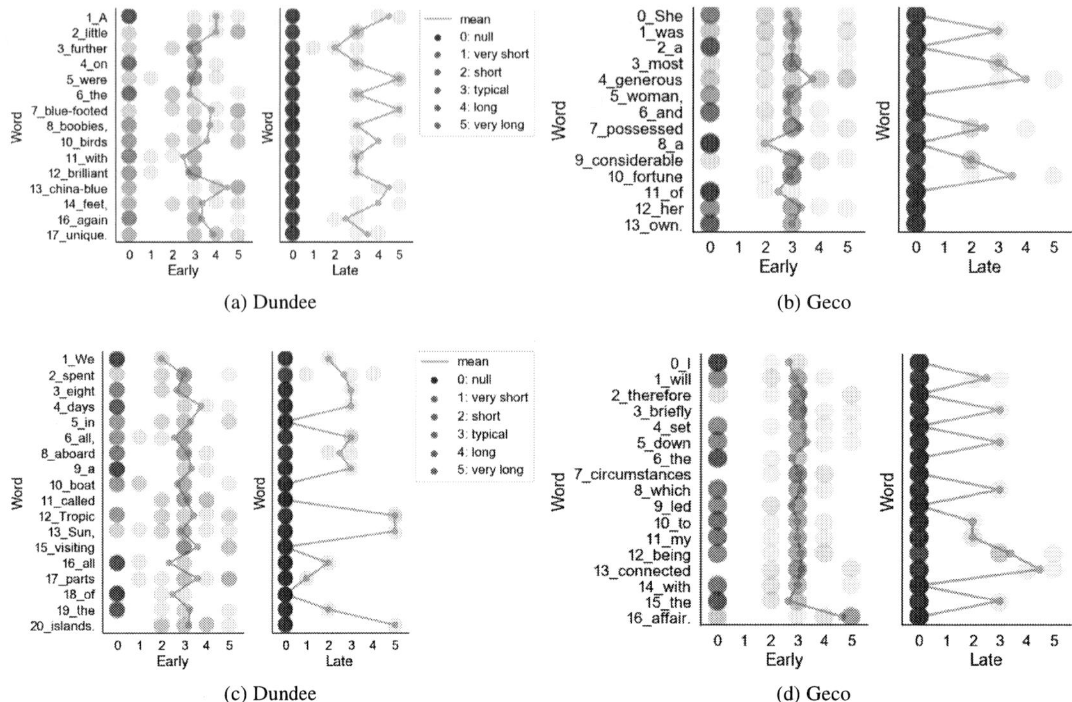

Figure 2: Example sentences from the two eye-tracking corpora.

by UD, which contains 12,543 sentences (204k tokens) for training, 2,002 sentences (25k tokens) for development and 2,077 sentences (25k tokens) for final evaluation. The development data is used for early stopping.

5.2 Model

In all our experiments, we use a bidirectional long short-term memory network (bi-LSTM) (Graves and Schmidhuber, 2005; Hochreiter and Schmidhuber, 1997; Plank et al., 2016) with a word encoding model which consists of a hierarchical model that combines pre-trained word embeddings with subword-character representations obtained from a recurrent character-based bi-LSTM.

For chunking and the MTL setup, we use the cascaded model proposed by (Klerke et al., 2016): it predicts the chunks at the outermost stacked-bi-LSTM layer of a 3-layer stacked network; and it predicts the gaze label at the first bi-LSTM layer. Note that our model differs from theirs in that we add a subword bi-LSTM at the character level, which has shown to be effective for POS tagging. Moreover, for POS we use a single bi-LSTM layer, hence the MTL setup reduces to a setup in which

both tasks are predicted from the the single bi-LSTM layer. For dictionary modeling, we use the model proposed by (Plank and Agić, 2018) which integrates type-level information as lexicon embeddings concatenated to the word and sub-word level representations.

Hyperparameters For both tasks we tune model parameters on the development data for the respective task. We keep word embedding inputs fixed, which are set to 64 (size of the pre-trained Polyglot embeddings). We tune LSTM dimensions, character representations and hidden dimensions on the dev data. Early stopping was important to avoid overfitting of the auxiliary task.[7]

For binary chunking, the hyperparameters are: character and hidden dimensions 64, hidden layer size 100, cascaded model for MTL. For POS tagging, the parameters are: character input and hid-

---

[7]The gaze representation splits the data into unbalanced classes. The preliminary results indicated a tendency for the multi-task setup auxiliary task to learn only the majority class. With the implementation of a patience threshold for early model stopping, this was eliminated in all but the local view of the late measure which coincides with the experiments where gaze data is most detrimental to target task performance.

Baseline		Token-level		Type-level	
		94.93			
		Early	Late	Early	Late
Dundee	G: mean	94.81	94.48	94.89	<u>94.94</u>
	G: var	94.78	94.67	**95.01**	**94.98**
	L: union	93.79	94.13	94.80	94.93
GECO	G: mean	94.61	94.70	<u>94.93</u>	94.80
	G: var	94.40	94.57	94.91	94.91
	L: union	94.06	93.87	94.74	94.93

Table 2: F1 scores for binary chunking task training with an early or late gaze metric as an auxiliary task or as a type-level lexicon. G: global, L: local. Underlined: above baseline. Best per early/late: boldfaced.

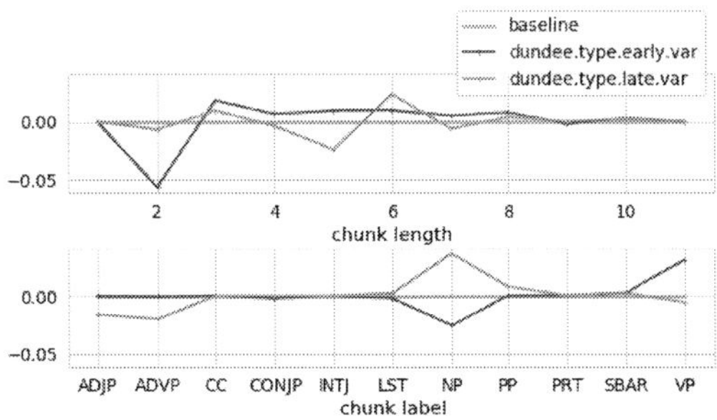

Figure 3: Relevance-weighted difference in F1 from baseline performance over chunk lengths and chunk labels for the Dundee data.

den dimension 64, hidden layer size 150. Both models were trained with Stochastic Gradient Decent (SGD) using a learning rate of 0.1, word dropout 0.25, and patience 2. The lexicon embedding size was tuned on Dundee data using the development data for both the Early and Late measure. For POS tagging the 40-dimensional lexical embeddings worked best for both Early and Late measure, similar to what was found for cross-lingual POS tagging (Plank and Agić, 2018). For chunking, the best result was obtained with 40 for Early and 70 for Late, respectively. In all experiments and tuning setups we average over 3 runs.

The chunking task is evaluated using phrase-based F1-score implemented by the conlleval script.[8] For POS tagging, performance is reported as tagging accuracy.

6 Results

6.1 Binary Phrase Chunking Results

Table 2 presents the results for the binary phrase chunking. Gaze data seems to provide little signal for this task. Over 2x12 setups, only the global (yet novel) view using variance at the type level provides a small increase in F1, but only on one gaze corpus.

Token vs type-level In more detail, for the chunking task the results show no benefit from learning gaze at token level in a multi-task setup (left two columns in Table 2). In all twelve MTL setups (two corpora, 2 gaze measures and three aggregations), no improvement is obtained over the baseline. In contrast, the type level dictionary-based gaze information is in all cases better than

the token-level MTL, yet, results largely fall below baseline. In one specific setup the novel variance aggregation way, which holds over both the early and the late measure, results in the best gaze-based model (boldface). It results in a modest improvement, but it is not robust: the specific setup only works for Dundee, it does not carry over to the Geco corpus. We return to these results below.

Global vs local What is interesting to note is a clear negative effect of using un-aggregated (local) data: The local view consistently fails to improve over the no-gaze baseline on the chunk boundary detection task. This is in marked contrast to results on sentence compression (Klerke et al., 2016) (where Dundee local union helped in addition to integrating CCG tagging). Here, keeping individual readers' gaze information confuses the model and taking an aggregated view is more beneficial.

Analysis To assess the impact of the experimental conditions, we compare the performance of the two best setups across chunk length and over the underlying kinds of chunks (by relating predicted binary chunks back to their original labeling). Figure 3 depict the differences between these two models as the difference in F1-score relative to the baseline and weighted by the proportion of data accounted for by each subgroup.

The figures show how differences in performance on medium length chunks separate the two best chunk boundary detection models, despite their overall similar performance (95.01 vs 94.98). Early performs worse on short chunks (2 words long), while this is the case for longer chunks (5 words) for the regression-based Late measure.

With respect to chunk label, there is an interesting difference in performance with respect to

---

[8]github.com/spyysalo/conlleval.py

chunk category: the early measure outperforms the baseline on VP's; the late measure outperforms it on NP's (for which the two result in near mirror images). Note that this difference in the Early and Late metric is observed despite the fact that the chunk type information was not part of training. This points to the importance of analyzing performance in more detail to reveal differences between overall similarly-performing models.

6.2 Part-of-Speech Tagging Results

Table 3 shows the results for Part-of-Speech tagging. In contrast to binary chunking, gaze data provides signal for supervised POS tagging. There are several take-aways.

Token vs type-level Integrating the gaze data as type-level dictionary is the most beneficial and aids Part-of-Speech tagging, more than multi-task learning does. In particular, for the dictionary-based approach, we observe improvements in 9 out of 12 cases, yielding to up to +.23 absolute accuracy improvement. This shows that gaze data aids POS tagging also in our high-resource supervised POS tagging setup, which complements earlier findings restricted to unsupervised POS induction with naturally lower baselines (Barrett and Søgaard, 2015a; Barrett et al., 2016). MTL leads to a few but not consistent improvements for POS.

Global vs local Again, using the globally aggregated gaze measures is better than taking the local view of the individual readers. For both Dundee and GECO corpora, results for the local view approach fall below baseline in almost all cases. This holds for the local view in both setups, dictionary and MTL.

Analysis We analyzed the types of tags for which we observed the most improvement (or drop) in performance on the best model per corpus relative to proportion in data. For Dundee (G: mean) we observe that the model using the Late measure improves the most on content tags (adj, nouns) and misses the most on function words (pron, sym). Similarly for Geco (Early) most improvements are observed for content words including subordinate conjunctions (adj, sconj) while largest drops are on pronouns and numerals.

7 Related Work and Discussion

Klerke et al. (2016) proposed the applicability of single gaze metrics for improving sentence com-

Baseline		Token-level		Type-level	
			95.25		
		Early	Late	Early	Late
Dundee	G: mean	<u>95.30</u>	<u>95.37</u>	**95.35**	**95.48**
	G: var	95.21	<u>95.33</u>	**95.35**	<u>95.44</u>
	L: union	95.01	95.23	<u>95.30</u>	95.17
GECO	G: mean	95.23	<u>95.27</u>	<u>95.34</u>	<u>95.35</u>
	G: var	<u>95.31</u>	95.22	<u>95.41</u>	95.23
	L: union	94.97	95.23	95.14	<u>95.26</u>

Table 3: Accuracy scores for POS tagging with an early or late gaze metric as type-level lexicon or as an auxiliary task. G: global aggregation, L: local. Underlined: above baseline. Best per measure: boldfaced.

pression. Using the first pass duration and a regression duration measure in a multi-task learning setup, their study is, to the best of our knowledge, the only one to report a benefit from using the un-aggregated (local) data. Our study contributes to this research lacuna, where our results show that un-aggregated data is inferior (RQ1)—the detrimental effect might be partly due to a possible higher noise-to-signal ratio, disfavoring such setups.

In contrast, Barrett and Søgaard (2015a) report benefits from aggregating the individual view of the data away, at first, and later demonstrate positive influence from aggregating also the individual tokens' context away, proposing the type-level view of gaze data for NLP (Barrett et al., 2016). Our results show that these type-level aggregates aid also supervised POS tagging, supporting further this type-level view. We here proposed a type-level view with novel global aggregation metrics and leveraging dictionary-based embeddings (Plank and Agić, 2018).

Recent related work on gaze in NLP rely to a greater extent on the strong emotional and affective gaze responses associated with the semantic content of a text. These works include the classification of sentiment (Mishra et al., 2017b; Hollenstein et al., 2019), coreferences (Jaffe et al., 2018; Cheri et al., 2016), named entities (Hollenstein and Zhang, 2019), sarcasm (Mishra et al., 2016) and multi-word detection (Yaneva et al., 2017; Rohanian et al., 2017).

8 Conclusions

We analyzed to which degree types of gaze aggregation over two distinct gaze measures impact on syntactic tagging.

Our results show that gaze data from a single feature is informative for supervised POS tagging, complementing previous findings on unsupervised POS induction. Results on binary phrase chunking are however largely negative; only one specific setup led to a modest improvement. This points to the importance of evaluating across tasks, aggregation method and gaze corpus.

In particular, we found (RQ1) that the local view of gaze interaction traces was not helpful in comparison to a global view of either the mean or the variance computed over multiple participants. We could observe a clear detrimental effect of the local view for both tasks. To the best of our knowledge, only one prior study report a benefit for this view (cf. Section 7).

Regarding RQ2, our results show that the type-level dictionary-based learning from an aggregated representation leads to better representations than the token-based multi-task learning setup. Overall, our results support that POS-tagging benefits more from the gaze signal than the simplified chunk-boundary detection task. Inspection of the best models further indicated that the improvement was based on particular sensitivity to content word classes and phrases. These observations collectively agree well with the emerging picture that particular aspects of some content words are reflected more reliably in gaze data, compared to less semantically rich aspects of text.

The two corpora we use show quite different results which may be an effect of a number of differences, pointing to important future directions of work. The difference in genre and typical sentence length and, not least in number of unique entities, as discussed in Hollenstein and Zhang (2019), would very likely have affected readers to optimize their reading strategy, and thereby their oculomotor program, accordingly. The distance in time and technological maturity is likely to have some effects as well, albeit those are less testable. Overall, our findings point to the importance of analyzing overall performance measures in more detail and evaluating impact across different corpora and NLP tasks.

Acknowledgments

The authors would like to thank the current and previous anonymous reviewers for their thorough reviews. This research has been supported by the Department of Computer Science at IT University of Copenhagen and NVIDIA cooperation.

References

Olivier Augereau, Kai Kunze, Hiroki Fujiyoshi, and Koichi Kise. 2016. Estimation of English skill with a mobile eye tracker. In *Proceedings of the 2016 ACM International Joint Conference on Pervasive and Ubiquitous Computing: Adjunct*, pages 1777–1781. ACM.

Maria Barrett, Joachim Bingel, Nora Hollenstein, Marek Rei, and Anders Søgaard. 2018a. Sequence classification with human attention. In *Proceedings of the 22nd Conference on Computational Natural Language Learning*, pages 302–312.

Maria Barrett, Joachim Bingel, Frank Keller, and Anders Søgaard. 2016. Weakly supervised part-of-speech tagging using eye-tracking data. In *Proceedings of the 54th Annual Meeting of the Association for Computational Linguistics*, volume 2, pages 579–584.

Maria Barrett, Ana Valeria Gonzlez-Garduo, Lea Frermann, and Anders Søgaard. 2018b. Unsupervised induction of linguistic categories with records of reading, speaking, and writing. In *Proceedings of the 2018 Conference of the North American Chapter of the Association for Computational Linguistics: Human Language Technologies*, volume 1, pages 2028–2038.

Maria Barrett and Anders Søgaard. 2015a. Reading behavior predicts syntactic categories. In *Proceedings of the nineteenth conference on computational natural language learning (CoNLL)*, pages 345–249.

Maria Barrett and Anders Søgaard. 2015b. Using reading behavior to predict grammatical functions. In *Proceedings of the Sixth Workshop on Cognitive Aspects of Computational Language Learning (CogACL)*, pages 1–5.

Mattias Nilsson Benfatto, Gustaf Öqvist Seimyr, Jan Ygge, Tony Pansell, Agneta Rydberg, and Christer Jacobson. 2016. Screening for dyslexia using eye tracking during reading. *PloS one*, 11(12):e0165508.

Joachim Bingel, Maria Barrett, and Sigrid Klerke. 2018. Predicting misreadings from gaze in children with reading difficulties. In *Proceedings of the Thirteenth Workshop on Innovative Use of NLP for Building Educational Applications*, pages 24–34.

Rich Caruana. 1997. Multitask learning. *Machine learning*, 28(1):41–75.

Joe Cheri, Abhijit Mishra, and Pushpak Bhattacharyya. 2016. Leveraging annotators' gaze behaviour for coreference resolution. In *Proceedings of the 7th Workshop on Cognitive Aspects of Computational*

Language Learning, pages 22–26, Berlin. Association for Computational Linguistics.

Agatha Christie. 1920. The mysterious affair at styles. 1920. *The Secret*.

Uschi Cop, Nicolas Dirix, Denis Drieghe, and Wouter Duyck. 2017. Presenting geco: An eyetracking corpus of monolingual and bilingual sentence reading. *Behavior research methods*, 49(2):602–615.

Vera Demberg and Frank Keller. 2008. Data from eyetracking corpora as evidence for theories of syntactic processing complexity. *Cognition*, 109(2):193–210.

Alex Graves and Jürgen Schmidhuber. 2005. Framewise phoneme classification with bidirectional lstm and other neural network architectures. *Neural Networks*, 18(5):602–610.

Sepp Hochreiter and Jürgen Schmidhuber. 1997. Long short-term memory. *Neural computation*, 9(8):1735–1780.

Nora Hollenstein, Maria Barrett, Marius Troendle, Francesco Bigiolli, Nicolas Langer, and Ce Zhang. 2019. Advancing nlp with cognitive language processing signals. *arXiv preprint arXiv:1904.02682*.

Nora Hollenstein and Ce Zhang. 2019. Entity recognition at first sight: Improving NER with eye movement information. In *Proceedings of the 2019 Conference of the North American Chapter of the Association for Computational Linguistics: Human Language Technologies, Volume 1 (Long and Short Papers)*, Minneapolis, Minnesota. Association for Computational Linguistics.

Kenneth Holmqvist, Marcus Nyström, Richard Andersson, Richard Dewhurst, Halszka Jarodzka, and Joost Van de Weijer. 2011. *Eye tracking: A comprehensive guide to methods and measures*. OUP Oxford.

Evan Jaffe, Cory Shain, and William Schuler. 2018. Coreference and focus in reading times. In *Proceedings of the 8th Workshop on Cognitive Modeling and Computational Linguistics (CMCL)*, pages 1–9.

Alan Kennedy, Robin Hill, and Joël Pynte. 2003. The Dundee Corpus. In *Proceedings of the 12th European conference on eye movement*.

Alan Kennedy and Joël Pynte. 2005. Parafoveal-on-foveal effects in normal reading. *Vision research*, 45(2):153–168.

Sigrid Klerke, Yoav Goldberg, and Anders Søgaard. 2016. Improving sentence compression by learning to predict gaze. In *Proceedings of 14th Annual Conference of the North American Chapter of the Association for Computational Linguistics (NAACL)*, pages 1528–1533.

Pascual Martínez-Gómez, Tadayoshi Hara, and Akiko Aizawa. 2012. Recognizing personal characteristics of readers using eye-movements and text features. *Proceedings of COLING 2012*, pages 1747–1762.

Franz Matthies and Anders Søgaard. 2013. With blinkers on: Robust prediction of eye movements across readers. In *Proceedings of the 2013 Conference on Empirical Methods in Natural Language Processing (EMNLP)*, pages 803–806, Seattle, Washington, USA.

Abhijit Mishra, Kuntal Dey, and Pushpak Bhattacharyya. 2017a. Learning cognitive features from gaze data for sentiment and sarcasm classification using convolutional neural network. In *Proceedings of the 55th Annual Meeting of the Association for Computational Linguistics (Volume 1: Long Papers)*, pages 377–387.

Abhijit Mishra, Kuntal Dey, and Pushpak Bhattacharyya. 2017b. Learning cognitive features from gaze data for sentiment and sarcasm classification using convolutional neural network. In *Proceedings of the 55th Annual Meeting of the Association for Computational Linguistics*, volume 1, pages 377–387.

Abhijit Mishra, Diptesh Kanojia, and Pushpak Bhattacharyya. 2016. Predicting readers' sarcasm understandability by modeling gaze behavior. In *AAAI*, pages 3747–3753.

Barbara Plank. 2016a. Keystroke dynamics as signal for shallow syntactic parsing. In *Proceedings of the 25th International Conference on Computational Linguistics (COLING)*, pages 609–618.

Barbara Plank. 2016b. What to do about non-standard (or non-canonical) language in NLP. *CoRR*, abs/1608.07836.

Barbara Plank and Željko Agić. 2018. Distant supervision from disparate sources for low-resource part-of-speech tagging. In *Proceedings of the 2018 Conference on Empirical Methods in Natural Language Processing*, pages 614–620, Brussels, Belgium. Association for Computational Linguistics.

Barbara Plank, Anders Søgaard, and Yoav Goldberg. 2016. Multilingual part-of-speech tagging with bidirectional long short-term memory models and auxiliary loss. In *Proceedings of the 54th Annual Meeting of the Association for Computational Linguistics (Volume 2: Short Papers)*, pages 412–418, Berlin, Germany. Association for Computational Linguistics.

Keith Rayner. 1998. Eye movements in reading and information processing: 20 years of research. *Psychological bulletin*, 124(3):372–422.

Keith Rayner, Kathryn H Chace, Timothy J Slattery, and Jane Ashby. 2006. Eye movements as reflections of comprehension processes in reading. *Scientific studies of reading*, 10(3):241–255.

Omid Rohanian, Shiva Taslimipoor, Victoria Yaneva, and Le An Ha. 2017. Using gaze data to predict multiword expressions. In *Proceedings of the International Conference Recent Advances in Natural Language Processing, RANLP*, pages 601–609.

Erik F Tjong Kim Sang and Sabine Buchholz. 2000. Introduction to the conll-2000 shared task chunking. In *Fourth Conference on Computational Natural Language Learning and the Second Learning Language in Logic Workshop*.

Titus von der Malsburg, Shravan Vasishth, and Reinhold Kliegl. 2012. Scanpaths in reading are informative about sentence processing. In *Proceedings of the First Workshop on Eye-tracking and Natural Language Processing*, pages 37–54.

Victoria Yaneva, Shiva Taslimipoor, Omid Rohanian, et al. 2017. Cognitive processing of multiword expressions in native and non-native speakers of english: Evidence from gaze data. In *International conference on computational and corpus-based phraseology*, pages 363–379. Springer.

Population based Seeded Self-Play for Compositional Language Learning

Abhinav Gupta[*]
MILA
abhinavg@nyu.edu

Ryan Lowe[*]
MILA
ryan.lowe@mail.mcgill.ca

Jakob Foerster
Facebook AI Research

Douwe Kiela
Facebook AI Research

Joelle Pineau
Facebook AI Research
MILA

Abstract

How can we teach artificial agents to use human language flexibly to solve problems in real-world environments? We have an example of this in nature: human babies eventually learn to use human language to solve problems, and they are taught with an adult human-in-the-loop. Unfortunately, current machine learning methods (e.g. from deep reinforcement learning) are too data inefficient to learn language in this way. An outstanding goal is finding an algorithm with a suitable 'language learning prior' that allows it to learn human language, while minimizing the number of on-policy human interactions. In this paper, we propose to learn such a prior in simulation using an approach we call, Learning to Learn to Communicate (L2C). Specifically, in L2C we train a meta-learning agent in simulation to interact with populations of pre-trained agents, each with their own distinct communication protocol. Once the meta-learning agent is able to quickly adapt to each population of agents, it can be deployed in new populations, including populations speaking human language. Our key insight is that such populations can be obtained via self-play, after pre-training agents with imitation learning on a small amount of off-policy human language data. We call this latter technique Seeded Self-Play (S2P). Our preliminary experiments show that agents trained with L2C and S2P need fewer on-policy samples to learn a compositional language in a Lewis signaling game.

1 Introduction

Language is one of the most important aspects of human intelligence; it allows humans to coordinate and share knowledge with each other. We will want artificial agents to understand language as it is a natural means for us to specify their goals.

So how can we train agents to understand language? We adopt the functional view of language (Wittgenstein, 1953) that has recently gained popularity (Lazaridou et al., 2016; Gauthier and Mordatch, 2016; Mordatch and Abbeel, 2017): agents understand language when they can use language to carry out tasks in the real world. One approach to training agents that can use language in their environment is via *emergent communication*, where researchers train randomly initialized agents to solve tasks requiring communication (Foerster et al., 2016; Lazaridou et al., 2018; Tieleman et al., 2018). An open question in emergent communication is how the resulting communication protocols can be transferred to learning human language (Baroni, 2019; Hupkes et al., 2019). Existing approaches attempt to do this using auxiliary tasks (Lee et al., 2018, 2017), for example having agents predict the label of an image in English while simultaneously playing an image-based referential game (Evtimova et al., 2017). While this works for learning the names of objects, it's unclear if simply using an auxiliary loss will scale to learning the English names of complex concepts, or learning to use English to interact in an grounded environment.

One approach that we know will work (eventually) for training language learning agents is using a human-in-the-loop, as this is how human babies acquire language. In other words, if we had a good enough model architecture and learning algorithm, the human-in-the-loop approach should work. However, recent work in this direction has concluded that current algorithms are too sample inefficient to effectively learn a language with compositional properties from humans (Chevalier-Boisvert et al., 2018). Human guidance is expensive, and thus we would want such an algorithm to be as sample efficient as possible. An open problem is thus to create an algorithm or training procedure that results in increased sample-efficiency for lan-

Proceedings of the Beyond Vision and LANguage: inTEgrating Real-world kNowledge (LANTERN), pages 62–66
Hong Kong, China, November 3, 2019. ©2019 Association for Computational Linguistics

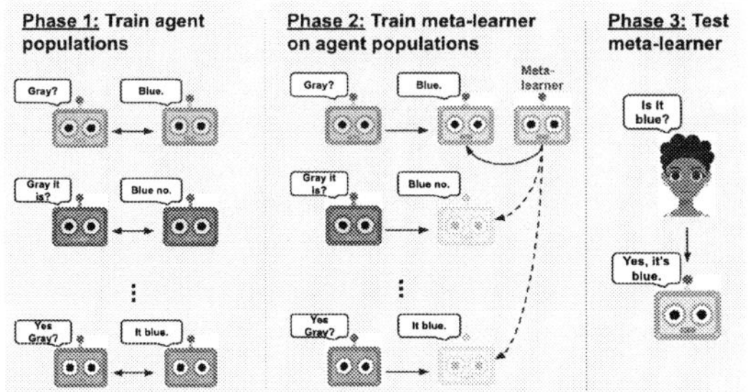

Figure 1: Schematic diagram of the L2C framework. An advantage of L2C is that agents can be trained in an external environment (which *grounds* the language), where agents interact with the environment via actions and language. Thus, (in theory) L2C could be scaled to learn complicated grounded tasks involving language.

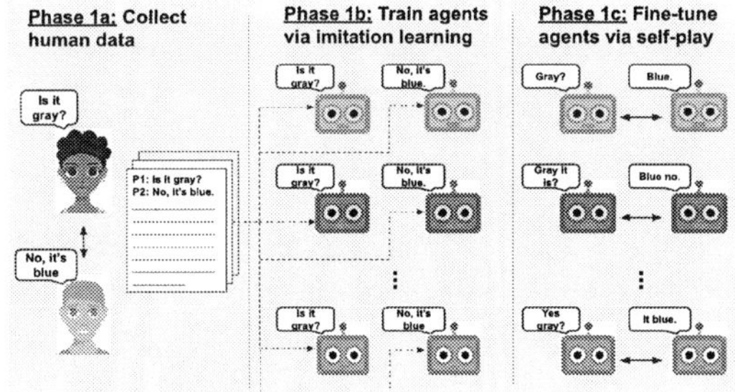

Figure 2: Schematic diagram of the S2P framework. Phase 1b and 1c are carried out in alternation or over some *schedule* to counter language drift while achieving high reward in the corresponding task. See Sec 3 for more details.

guage learning with a human-in-the-loop.

In this paper, we present the Learning to Learn to Communicate (L2C) framework, with the goal of training agents to quickly learn new (human) languages. The core idea behind L2C is to leverage the increasing amount of available compute for machine learning experiments (Amodei and Hernandez, 2018) to learn a 'language learning prior' by training agents via meta-learning in simulation. Specifically, we train a meta-learning agent in simulation to interact with populations of pre-trained agents, each with their own distinct communication protocol. Once the meta-learning agent is able to quickly adapt to each population of agents, it can be deployed in new populations unseen during training, including populations of humans. The L2C framework has two main advantages: (1) permits for agents to learn language that is *grounded* in an environment with which the agents can *interact* (i.e. it is not limited to referential games); and (2) in contrast with work from the instruction following literature (Bahdanau et al., 2018), agents can be trained via L2C to both *speak* (output language to help accomplish their goal) and *listen* (map from the language to a goal or sequence of actions).

To show the promise of the L2C framework, we provide some preliminary experiments in a Lewis signaling game (David, 1969). Specifically, we show that agents trained with L2C are able to learn a simple form of human language (represented by a hand-coded compositional language) in fewer iterations than randomly initialized agents. These preliminary results suggest that L2C is a promising framework for training agents to learn human language from few human interactions.

2 Learning to learn to communicate

L2C is a training procedure that is composed of three main phases: (1) **Training agent populations:** Training populations of agents to solve some task (or set of tasks) in an environment. (2) **Train meta-learner on agent populations:** We train a meta-learning agent to 'perform well' (i.e. achieve a high reward) on tasks in each of the training populations, after a small number of updates. (3) **Testing the meta-learner:** testing the meta-learning agent's ability to learn new languages, which could be both artificial (emerged languages unseen during training) or human.

A diagram giving an overview of the L2C framework is shown in Figure 1. Phase 1 can be achieved in any number of ways, either through supervised learning (using approximate backpropogation) or via reinforcement learning (RL). Phases 2 and 3 follow the typical meta-learning set-up: to conserve space, we do not replicate a formal description of the meta-learning framework, but we direct interested readers to Section 2.1 of (Finn et al., 2017). In our case, each 'task' involves a separate population of agents with its own emergent language. While meta-training can also be performed via supervised learning or RL, Phase 3 must be done using RL, as it involves interacting with humans which cannot be differentiated through.

3 Seeded self-play

Seeded self-play (S2P) is a straightforward technique for training agents in simulation to develop complex behaviours. The idea is to 'seed' a population of agents and use that data to train other populations. Fig 2 gives a pictorial representation

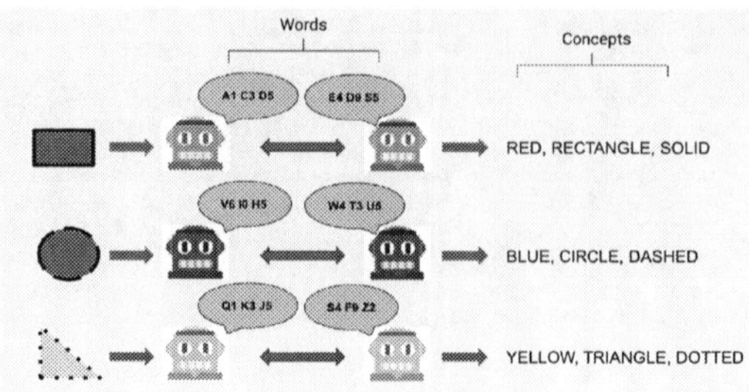

Figure 3: Lewis Signalling game with 2 agents, a Speaker and a Listener. For more details refer to Sec 4.

of S2P.

We collect some data which is sampled from a fixed seed population. This corresponds to the actual number of samples that we care about which is basically the number of human demonstrations. We first train each agent (a listener and a speaker) that performs well on these human samples. We call this step as the *imitation-learning* step. Then we take each of these trained agents (a pair of speaker and a listener) and deploy them against each other to solve the task via emergent communication. We call this step as the *fine-tuning* step. While these agents are exchanging messages in their emergent language, we make sure that the language does not diverge too much form the original language (i.e. the language of the fixed seed population). We enforce this by having a schedule over the *fine-tuning* and the *imitation-learning* steps such that both the agents are able to solve the task while also keeping a perfect accuracy over the seed data. We call this process of generating populations as *seeded self-play* (S2P).

4 Problem set-up

A speaker-listener game We construct a referential game similar to the Task & Talk game from (Kottur et al., 2017), except with a single turn. The game is cooperative and consists of 2 agents, a speaker and a listener. The speaker agent observes an object with a certain set of properties, and must describe the object to the listener using a sequence of words (represented by one-hot vectors). The listener then attempts to reconstruct the object. More specifically, the input space consists of p *properties* (e.g. shape, color) and t *types* per property (e.g. triangle, square). The speaker observes a symbolic representation of the input x, consisting of the concatenation of p one-hot vectors, each of length t. The number of possible inputs scales as t^p. We

define the vocabulary size (length of each one-hot vector sent from the speaker) as $|V|$, and fix the number of words sent to be w.

Developing a compositional language To simulate a simplified form of human language on this task, we programatically generate a perfectly compositional language, by assigning each 'concept' (each type of each property) a unique symbol. In other words, to describe a blue shaded triangle, we create a language where the output description would be "blue, triangle, shaded", in some arbitrary order and without prepositions. By 'unique symbol', we mean that no two concepts are assigned the same word. We call these agents speaking compositional language as *Compositional Bots*. By generating this language programmatically, we avoid the need to have humans in the loop for testing, which allows us to iterate much more quickly. This is feasible because of the simplicity of our speaker-listener environment; we do not expect that generating these programmatic languages is practical when scaling to more complex environments.

Implementation details The speaker and listener are parameterized by recurrent policies, both using an embedding layer of size 200 followed by an LSTM of size 200. Both the speaker and the listener agents use the same number of parameters for encoding/decoding the message. The message produced by the speaker is a sequence of p categorical random variables which are discretized using Gumbel-Softmax relaxation (Jang et al., 2016; Maddison et al., 2016) with an initial temperature $\tau = 1$ which is annealed over a schedule with $\gamma = 0.7$ for every 10000 iterations. We set the vocabulary size to be equal to the total number of concepts $p \cdot t$. In our initial experiments, we train our agents using Cross Entropy which is summed over each property p. We use the Adam optimizer (Kingma and Ba, 2015) with a learning rate of 0.001 and a scheduler which anneals the learning rate with a $\gamma = 0.5$. We first demonstrate the results with a meta-learning listener (a *meta-listener*), that learns from the different speakers of each training population.

5 Experiments

5.1 Meta-learning improves sample efficiency

Here, we describe our initial results into the factors affecting the performance of L2C. Since our ultimate goal is to transfer to learning a human

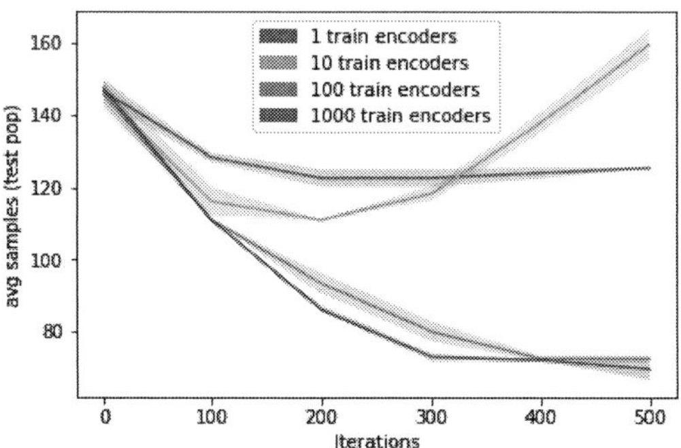

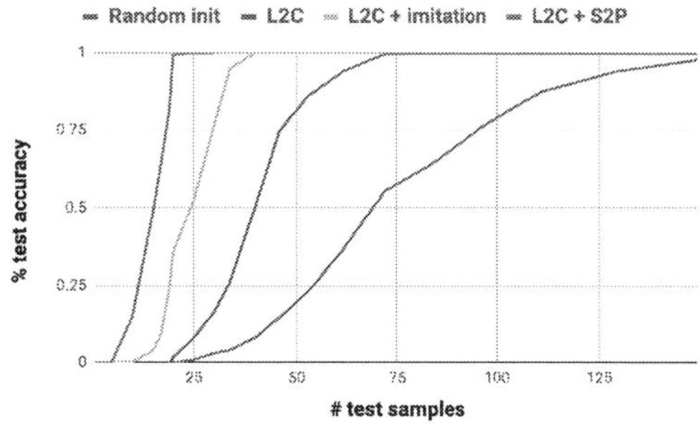

Figure 5: Varying performance across different number of test samples for all combinations of proposed frameworks. L2C+S2P performs the best, only needing 20 samples as compared to the 60 samples for L2C and 150 samples for randomly initialized agent.

Figure 4: Performance of the meta-learner (in terms of number of training samples required to achieve >95% test accuracy on a test population) over the course of meta-training (horizontal axis), while varying the number of training encoders. Results averaged over 5 seeds, with standard error shown. Note the vertical axis is in log scale.

language in as few human interactions as possible, we measure success based on the number of samples required for the meta-learner to reach a certain performance level (95%) on a held-out test population, and we permit ourselves as much computation during pre-training as necessary.

As can be inferred from Figure 4, having more training populations improves performance. Having too few training populations (eg: 5 train encoders) results in overfitting to the set of training populations and as the meta-learning progresses, the model performs worse on the test populations. For more than 10 training encoders, models trained with L2C require fewer samples to generalize to a held-out test population than a model not trained with L2C.

5.2 Self-play improves sample efficiency

We wanted to see if we can further reduce the number of samples required after L2C. So instead of doing L2C on a population of compositional bots, we train the population of agents using Seeded self-play (S2P). We collect some seed data from a single compositional bot which we call as *seed dataset*. Now we partition this data into train and test sets where the train set is used to train the agents via S2P. This set of trained populations is now used as the set of populations for meta-training (L2C). Fig 5 compares the results of populations trained via S2P and the compositional bots. It is evident that we need 40 fewer samples to generalize on the test set, when the populations are trained via S2P

than using hard-coded bots.

6 Outstanding challenges

There are several immediate directions for future work: training the meta-agent via RL rather than supervised learning, and training the meta-agent as a joint speaker-listener (i.e. taking turns speaking and listening), as opposed to only listening. We also want to scale L2C training to more complicated tasks involving grounded language learning, such as the Talk the Walk dataset (de Vries et al., 2018), which involves two agents learning to navigate New York using language.

More broadly, there are still many challenges that remain for the L2C framework. In fact, there are unique problems that face each of the phases described in Section 2. In Phase 1, how do we know we can train agents to solve the tasks we want? Recent work has shown that learning emergent communication protocols is very difficult, even for simple tasks (Lowe et al., 2017). This is particularly true in the multi-agent reinforcement learning (RL) setting, where deciding on a communication protocol is difficult due to the non-stationary and high variance of the gradients (Lowe et al., 2017). This could be addressed in at least two ways: (1) by assuming the environment is differentiable, and backpropagating gradients using a stochastic differentiation procedure (Jang et al., 2016; Mordatch and Abbeel, 2017), or (2) by 'seeding' each population with a small number of human demonstrations. Point (1) is feasible because we are training in simulation, and we have control over how we build that simulation — in short, it doesn't really matter *how* we get our trained agent populations, so long as they are useful for the meta-learner in Phase 2.

In Phase 2, the most pertinent question is: how can we be sure that a small number of updates is sufficient for a meta-agent to learn a language it has never seen before? The short answer is that it doesn't need to completely learn the language in only a few updates; rather it just needs to perform better on the language-task in the host population after a few updates, in order to provide a useful training signal to the meta-learner. For instance, it has been shown that the model agnostic meta-learning (MAML) algorithm can perform well when multiple gradient steps are taken at test time, even if it is only trained with a single inner gradient step. Another way to improve the meta-learner performance is to provide a *dataset* of agent interactions for each population. In other words, rather than needing to meta-learner perform well after interacting with a population a few times, we'd like it to perform well after doing some supervised learning on this dataset of language, and after a few interactions. After all, we do have lots of available datasets of human language, and not using this seems like a waste.

References

Amodei, D. and Hernandez, D. (2018). Ai and compute. *https://blog. openai. com/aiand-compute*.

Bahdanau, D., Hill, F., Leike, J., Hughes, E., Kohli, P., and Grefenstette, E. (2018). Learning to follow language instructions with adversarial reward induction. *arXiv preprint arXiv:1806.01946*.

Baroni, M. (2019). Linguistic generalization and compositionality in modern artificial neural networks.

Chevalier-Boisvert, M., Bahdanau, D., Lahlou, S., Willems, L., Saharia, C., Nguyen, T. H., and Bengio, Y. (2018). Babyai: First steps towards grounded language learning with a human in the loop. *arXiv preprint arXiv:1810.08272*.

David, L. (1969). Convention: a philosophical study.

de Vries, H., Shuster, K., Batra, D., Parikh, D., Weston, J., and Kiela, D. (2018). Talk the walk: Navigating new york city through grounded dialogue. *arXiv preprint arXiv:1807.03367*.

Evtimova, K., Drozdov, A., Kiela, D., and Cho, K. (2017). Emergent Communication in a Multi-Modal, Multi-Step Referential Game. page 13.

Finn, C., Abbeel, P., and Levine, S. (2017). Model-agnostic meta-learning for fast adaptation of deep networks. *arXiv preprint arXiv:1703.03400*.

Foerster, J. N., Assael, Y. M., de Freitas, N., and Whiteson, S. (2016). Learning to communicate with deep multi-agent reinforcement learning. *CoRR*, abs/1605.06676.

Gauthier, J. and Mordatch, I. (2016). A paradigm for situated and goal-driven language learning. *arXiv preprint arXiv:1610.03585*.

Hupkes, D., Dankers, V., Mul, M., and Bruni, E. (2019). The compositionality of neural networks: integrating symbolism and connectionism. *arXiv:1908.08351 [cs, stat]*. arXiv: 1908.08351.

Jang, E., Gu, S., and Poole, B. (2016). Categorical reparameterization with gumbel-softmax. *arXiv preprint arXiv:1611.01144*.

Kingma, D. P. and Ba, J. (2015). Adam: A method for stochastic optimization. *CoRR*, abs/1412.6980.

Kottur, S., Moura, J. M., Lee, S., and Batra, D. (2017). Natural language does not emerge'naturally'in multi-agent dialog. *arXiv preprint arXiv:1706.08502*.

Lazaridou, A., Hermann, K. M., Tuyls, K., and Clark, S. (2018). Emergence Of Linguistic Communication From Referential Games With Symbolic And Pixel. page 13.

Lazaridou, A., Peysakhovich, A., and Baroni, M. (2016). Multi-agent cooperation and the emergence of (natural) language. *arXiv preprint arXiv:1612.07182*.

Lee, J., Cho, K., and Kiela, D. (2018). Countering language drift via grounding.

Lee, J., Cho, K., Weston, J., and Kiela, D. (2017). Emergent Translation in Multi-Agent Communication. *arXiv:1710.06922 [cs]*. arXiv: 1710.06922.

Lowe, R., Wu, Y., Tamar, A., Harb, J., Abbeel, O. P., and Mordatch, I. (2017). Multi-agent actor-critic for mixed cooperative-competitive environments. In *Advances in Neural Information Processing Systems*, pages 6379–6390.

Maddison, C. J., Mnih, A., and Teh, Y. W. (2016). The concrete distribution: A continuous relaxation of discrete random variables. *arXiv preprint arXiv:1611.00712*.

Mordatch, I. and Abbeel, P. (2017). Emergence of grounded compositional language in multi-agent populations. *arXiv preprint arXiv:1703.04908*.

Tieleman, O., Lazaridou, A., Mourad, S., Blundell, C., and Precup, D. (2018). Shaping representations through communication. *OpenReview*.

Wittgenstein, L. (1953). Philosophical investigations.

Author Index

Association for Computational Linguistics
209 N. Eighth Street
Stroudsburg, Pennsylvania 18360

ISBN 978-1-7138-0082-8